Lambert De Boilieu

Recollections of Labrador life

Lambert De Boilieu

Recollections of Labrador life

ISBN/EAN: 9783741173912

Manufactured in Europe, USA, Canada, Australia, Japa

Cover: Foto ©Andreas Hilbeck / pixelio.de

Manufactured and distributed by brebook publishing software (www.brebook.com)

Lambert De Boilieu

Recollections of Labrador life

CONTENTS.

CHAPTER I.
THE PASSAGE OUT .. .. .. 9 (PAGE)

CHAPTER II.
IN HARBOUR 21

CHAPTER III.
COD CATCHING AND CURING 32

CHAPTER IV.
LIFE ON THE ISLAND 43

CHAPTER V.
BEARS—BLACK AND WHITE 52

CHAPTER VI.
WOLVES, DEER, GAME, ETC. 63

CONTENTS.

CHAPTER VII.
Fur Animals and Seals 75

CHAPTER VIII.
Seals 89

CHAPTER IX.
Winter—Christmas 101

CHAPTER X.
The Woods—Woodhouses, etc. 115

CHAPTER XI.
The Esquimaux 124

CHAPTER XII.
Adventures—Fox-trapping 140

CHAPTER XIII.
Spring, Spring-Ducks, etc. 153

CHAPTER XIV.
Foxes—Tales—Sea—Tracks .. 171

CHAPTER XV.

Newfoundland and Back Again 181

CHAPTER XVI.

Life on the Coast—Autumn 188

CHAPTER XVII.

King Frost Again 197

CHAPTER XVIII.

Expedition to Sandwich Bay 209

CHAPTER XIX.

Journey Home from Sandwich Bay 222

CHAPTER XX.

Home Again 232

CHAPTER XXI.

Trained Dogs, and Homeward Bound 239

RECOLLECTIONS

OF

LABRADOR LIFE.

CHAPTER I.

THE PASSAGE OUT.

I REMEMBER that fine crisp morning in the month of May, when I left my home bent on seeking my fortune in a strange land. I was not at all particular as to which part of the globe I should visit; so taking a westerly course from the Great City, I found myself in a few days at a small seaport town in Devon, and there I embarked on my first voyage to a country known only to me by name. Without further preface, it was a voyage to Labrador. The ship I embarked in was a snug little brig of 200 tons' register. We had fine weather for several days down Channel, but, notwithstanding this, it seemed that my adventures were to begin already. About 3 A.M. on the 29th May, one of the youngsters of the brig, a few years my junior, happened to slip overboard from the head. Knowing he could not swim, I—who was a good swimmer—did not hesitate, but leapt into the water and, after some little difficulty, saved him. Here, I take it, is a decided proof of the desirability of all boys being taught, when young, to swim, for when I first began to acquire the accomplishment, I had no notion I should ever find it of much practical service.

My next adventure—or, rather, this was the brig's adventure—occurred early one morning, when I was strangely impressed and somewhat frightened by hearing "the man at the mast-head" crying out, "Iceberg ahead!" On going aloft to look at it, I could only see a small speck on the horizon, but this, I was told by the man on the look-out, was the berg, and that it was a very large one. It was about four miles off, and the wind being extremely light, it was some hours before we were abreast of it. I can give but a poor description of the grandeur of the berg. It seemed to me like a large city with innumerable church-steeples rising here and there. In size, I was told, it was from four to five miles long, and about one mile broad, so that it really might, in this particular, have been a city, and held a city's population; subsequently I saw bergs even larger and broader. To be in the vicinity of an iceberg, I may seize occasion to remark here, is very dangerous for a ship, as the course of the mass of ice is not direct but "circular," and if an unfortunate ship should chance to get into its vortex, she becomes numbered with those that are eventually returned as missing.

After passing the iceberg we encountered some rough weather, which the master attributed—rightly enough, as we subsequently found—to our being in the vicinity of the main jam of ice. A "jam of ice" was his own expressive phrase,—indeed, a better name could not be given to it,—and its deafening, innumerous noise was terrible. It seemed to me then—and I cannot think of a better comparison now—as if two parks of artillery were blazing away one against the other. The wind speedily began to freshen, and then came the trial for the master and sailors. Almost at one breath the words were shouted to the man at the helm, "hard up," "hard down," and in less than another minute all hands had jumped out on the ice-pans to clear the ice from the brig's bow. "Well," I thought, "if this lasts long, it will prove the master of the whole of us." Fortunately, however, as night came on the wind lulled, and left us nearly becalmed, which, after the continuous roar of the preceding day, seemed all the more solemn.

As we lay upon the water we could see here and there a solitary seal, or perchance a wild fowl popping its head above the broken ice; but with the exception of this for three days, during which time we were becalmed, we saw nothing worth noticing. All that time the man on the look-out was straining his eyes to catch a glimpse of clear water, or to speak more plainly a passage through the "jam," and straining them in vain.

Now it happened that the master of the brig was an "old hand" on the coast, and knew perfectly well what every appearance of the atmosphere indicated; and on the fourth day he hailed the man on the look-out, and asked him if he saw any fog-banks, and, if he did, in what direction they were. The man answered that he did see a fog-bank lying to the north-west. Being curious to learn to what the master's question had reference, I inquired of him, when, in a simple, kindly way, he explained the whole matter to me. "Where," said he, "the ice is in large quantities, the fog won't rise, as it is absorbed as fast as it is generated. It's very different, though," he added, "with clear water. There the fog rises. We may certainly find a few pans of ice out there, where the fog is; but nothing to speak of."

The old master then gave orders for the

brig's head to be turned to the north-west, and after great exertion on the part of the crew we found ourselves, about eight hours after, in a clear channel, say about a quarter of a mile wide, which was quite enough to turn the brig to windward in. From certain movements or "indications" on the part of the bird, known on the coast as the Barcaliau bird,—that is to say, from its flying the whole day in the same direction,—we knew it was migrating to the Funk or Bird Island for the purpose of breeding. Formerly the island swarmed with penguins, and, for the sake of their feathers, the Newfoundlanders used to frequent the place in the spring of the year and destroy the birds in myriads. The island being quite barren, recourse was had to the bird even for fuel. I must explain this: in the north, where large quantities of birds are killed, the ordinary mode of stripping them of their feathers is not pursued, but a large boiler of hot water is employed, in which the birds, after being killed, are dipped one at a time, and then the feathers are easily *rubbed* off. Now the Newfoundlanders burnt the penguins to keep the pot boiling, and thus, in a short space of time, exterminated the whole breed from the coast.

On the day following our release from the ice, we came within sight of Belle Isle, and there found a clear passage to the northward. The weather was fine in the extreme (the fog having entirely cleared away), and we had an uninterrupted view of the bold coast of Labrador. To my mind it looked like one vast fortification, the ice being of a uniform wall-like appearance all along the rocky shore; that is to say, it was some fifteen feet high by about ten feet thick. While I was looking, one of the sailors called my attention to an extraordinary conflict which was taking place, not more than thirty yards from the ship, between three " monsters of the deep." The water being smooth and clear, I could perfectly distinguish all their movements. The first of the three " monsters " I saw was the whale, and in pursuit of this, apparently acting in concert, were the sword-fish and thresher. The mode of warfare adopted by the two last was singular and ingenious. The sword-fish would watch for the whale when he came up to the surface to blow, when he would quickly dive under him; the thresher, however, remained upon the surface, and did his part "above water," which was to "thresh" the whale with his tail, and force him down on the point of the sword-fish. How long the chase had lasted before we hove in sight of them we could not say, but in about ten minutes we saw the water was discoloured, and then the whale disappeared. No doubt the coalition had triumphed.

It is only in sailing ships such an extraordinary conflict could have been witnessed: a steamer would have disturbed the water and driven the fish away long before it had reached the field of battle.

For one day more we were striving to gain our port, which, I should remark, was only a few miles distant, during which time I had an opportunity of contemplating the cold and colossal grandeur of the scene around us. Innumerable icebergs of all sizes and forms, some representing large buildings, some like ancient churches, and some like old-world monuments, were to be seen on every hand, and over all bent a clear crystalline sky. One "casualty," which nearly proved fatal to the whole of us, occurred before we got into harbour. I must here state, what I have little doubt has been often *before* stated in Polar narratives,—that the icebergs are of various depths, and should the mass hidden below the water come in contact with a shoal, it breaks off; the "top-heavy" mass then turns over (like, to compare the very great with the very small, a child's sap-tumbler), and what was the top becomes the bottom. In turning over, however, quantities of loose ice split, snap, and splinter away, and thus it was in the present instance. First, as the berg began to roll over, we heard a low rumbling noise like muttered thunder; then, this swelled and seemed to come nearer and nearer; and then, as the mass really toppled and fell, there was a tremendous crash *against* the water, and hundreds of tons of *débris* were thrown high up into the air. Fortunately we were just beyond this "hurtling shower" of ice, or the result would have been fatal to craft and crew. The next day saw us snug in a small harbour on the coast of Labrador.

CHAPTER II.

IN HARBOUR.

The 25th June, and all around me nothing but ice and snow, with the sun shining beautifully overhead! I could scarce believe I was in a place inhabited by human beings. A sort of deathlike stillness seemed to reign over the snow, and there was no land in sight, so far as I could make out. I was told the snow was thawing fast, although I could not at first perceive it. On close examination, however, I found this to be the case, and also found that on the Labrador coast the snow thaws from the ground, and not from the surface.

I was much surprised that in about ten days after my arrival, things began to put on a spring-like appearance. The snow had left us, land was to be seen, and the sun shone with an undimmed lustre. Still I could see no vegetation whatever around me; all was bright, barren, and bare. The island I was located on was about two miles long and one broad, inhabited by only about sixty persons in the winter, but in the summer by some thousands. I found the men busy preparing for the toil of summer—fishing; for directly the ice leaves the coast, shoals of cod make their appearance, to deposit their spawn in the quiet bays with which the seaboard abounds.

The first Sunday I passed on shore, I seized occasion to ask a few questions respecting the missionaries I had heard had done so much in this (as in every other) part of the world.

The information I received somewhat astonished me, for on my asking one of the old hands if he had seen many missionaries during the time he had been living there, his reply was, as near as possible, as follows:—

"The fact is this 'ere place is too poor for 'um to come to; we havn't furs enough for them, and they can't set up 'shop' here. Why, do you know," he added, half-indignantly, "I went down a winter or two ago to the 'Arabian Nights' Territory,' to try and trade with the North-west Indians; well, would you believe it, when I came up with them I was positively driven away, as they said they were forbidden to trade with any other but the Arabian Nights."

I was curious to know who the Arabian Nights (? knights) were, and asked him for an explanation; but, from his supreme ignorance, I could get nothing more than a repetition of the same, to me, unmeaning phrase. Some time afterwards, however, I discovered it was the name given to some missionaries who had established themselves in the richest part of the coast, abounding in valuable furs of all descriptions; and I further found the place where I then was had not been visited by any mission for years, and I am somewhat doubtful if it ever had. I mean by the "missionaries," those of the Established Church, or Dissenters; the Roman Catholic missions I saw every year, and they remained with their flock about two months each summer-time. I wrote to the Bishop of Nova Scotia, and pointed out to him the state of affairs for some hundreds of miles along the coast, asking him for a trifle towards erecting a small chapel, in which, when built, I offered—as there was no one else at hand—my services to read prayers and give lectures. The prelate, however, politely declined to assist me in any way. Still, during the time I lived on the coast, when opportunities offered, I read prayers to an assembled few. To me it seems sad and shameful that a large district adjoining, I may say, Nova Scotia, should be without all spiritual administration; that people should be " married," christened, and in some parts buried, without rite or service of religion being performed. So much for our boast of missionaries, and our dissemination of the Gospel in foreign parts! The furs really outweigh the faith.

I must now proceed, however, to more mundane affairs, and attempt a description of the ordinary life and regular routine of the place. The cargo generally taken out from England consists of salt (ballast), which is used for the purpose of curing the fish; dry goods and provisions are also exported from home. The cargo unloaded and stored, the crews are divided in parties of three or four men, each being titled according to the position he holds in the boat. For instance, "skipper," "second hand," "midshipman;" last comes the "captain," who has the least to do—merely, indeed, to cook for the rest and to keep the boat clean. Every day brings its cargoes of Irish, who migrate here in the summer to catch fish, cure it, and take it back with them in the fall of the year, and dispose of it either in Newfoundland, or proceed with it to the markets of Genoa or Leghorn. Now, in the summer season, commences an active, bustling scene; every person is employed night and day in obtaining fish. I say night, but it is night merely in name. Night and day hold each other's hands upon the hill-tops; which in plain prose is,—no sooner does the sun set north by west, than, like a giant refreshed, it rises again north by east, having been absent only about an hour. Such a sudden change must be seen to be adequately appreciated, or even fully understood. Imagine an artist painting sunrise and sunset from nature at the same time, the lights and shades of "daybreak" and "evening" absolutely mingling together about an object!

Go on the hill with your spyglass, and look around; never was a more glorious sight! What a month ago was one chill ruin of ice— "a marble storm in monumental rage"—now teems with life and placid natural beauty. You may observe some two hundred boats or more on the Fishing Ground, the occupants sitting, still and dark, against the clear, sparkling atmosphere. A perfect harmony is kept up between the whole of the fraternity of fishermen; you seldom hear of them quarrelling. They are now, as you look, waiting for each other to cast their nets, for they like to act in unison. Some of these nets are formidable machines, being about two hundred and forty fathoms long, by from eighty to ninety fathoms deep. I have seen one of them quite full of cod-fish, when, in drawing it up, a small rent was found to have been made in it, and the fish—finding this out too—made their escape, not a single one being caught. When a good haul is made a signal is hoisted, and all spare hands are employed to fetch the fish home. Besides the large " seine," each boat is provided with five or six nets, to place the fish in when caught; these nets will hold from one to three tons. They are filled from the large net, and moored in the neighbourhood of the hauling-place, a watch-buoy, with the owner's name upon it, being set floating on the water. A boat from the fishing establishment or depôt having arrived alongside one of these, the work of loading the jack (by which name all boats attending the seine are called) is soon completed, and the fish are brought home and unloaded. The mode of unloading may here be described. The fish are not taken out by hand, but by an instrument called a " pew," which is a prong with one point. Should a fish be damaged in the body, it is deteriorated in value; so great care is taken to stick the pew through the head of the cod, and thus to land it on the stage-head, where it undergoes the first process of salting. In large establishments the cod-stage is usually a permanent building built over the water, with generally a good depth of water in front, in which is cast the offal of the fish. The size of the stage varies from one hundred to one hundred and fifty feet long, by about thirty feet wide. At the end, near the water, is a long table, set crossways, and the end of the stage itself is like an ordinary store, with folding-doors opening from the waterside. The fish being all landed, the operation of salting commences, and no one ever thinks of leaving off work until the whole haul of fish is cleared and salted in bulk. The first person on the stage engaged in curing fish is the "cut-throat," with his double-edged knife; the next is the "header," who dislocates the neck, and forces the head of the fish off, which falls into the water through a hole cut in the table. The header also separates the liver, which likewise passes through the table into a tub placed for its reception. The fish is then handed over to the "splitter," who opens it to the tail, and, with one smart and sharp blow from a splitting knife, separates the backbone. If this process is well done, the end where the first incision was made represents the figure 8; and the splitters plume themselves on (without intending any joke) their *eightful* skill. The fish is next placed on a sledge, or sliding barrow, and taken away by the principal actor on the stage—the person who cures or salts. The cod is now placed in what is called salt-bulk, where it may remain any period of time; for, so long as fish is being caught in the bay, so long will the "drying" and "washing"—which constitute the final process—be delayed.

CHAPTER III.

COD CATCHING AND CURING.

Continuing my notes piscatorial, I may commence this chapter by informing the reader that the man who prosecutes, or speculates in, the fishery, is called the Planter; and his mode is generally to hire his men by the voyage, giving them food and lodging, with the use of a boat, for half their labour, retaining, however, the cod-livers for himself. Under this arrangement a good hand will clear in about three months from twenty-five to thirty pounds. Strange to say, each man knows his own fish, the method of marking them being this:—Suppose three men are fishing together,—one cuts a notch on the right side of the tail, the second cuts one on the left, and the third leaves his as he catches them. When the fish are cured, each man selects his own by the mark. With the cod-fish comes the caplin fish (*Salmo Arcticus*), in such shoals that it is extremely difficult to row a boat through them. The fishermen use them as bait with which to catch the cod. The whale, too, is very fond of the caplin, and annually destroys them in thousands. I recollect once being employed in procuring this bait when it was scarce, and having found some in a small inlet, I obtained a boat-load and was about returning homeward, when our passage out of the inlet or cove was disputed by a whale, who, attracted by the caplin, was disappointed at our first capture, and kept us at bay nearly two hours. We had no fire-arms in the boat, or I have a shrewd notion that the two hours would have been lessened. It was not pleasant to find the way stopped by such a monster. It may seem strange that the caplin should come so close in-shore, as if for the very purpose of losing its life. It looks very much like *felo de se*, but the fact is, the female caplin is a small, slender, and weak fish, without sufficient power to emit her spawn, unless assisted by the male. Let me explain: On a fine day, when there is a light ripple on the beach, you may see thousands of these beautiful small female fishes swimming towards the shore or landwash, each accompanied by two males, one on each side of her; nearing the sand, the males press against the female, when the spawn is rapidly deposited. In nine cases out of ten, however, some of the party lose their lives, as they dart on shore so swiftly, that the ripple retires without bearing them back.

When caplin is scarce, recourse is had to another small fish, called the lance or sand-eel, for bait. Great toil and labour are experienced in procuring this fish; men sometimes being away for days before a sufficient supply can be obtained for a half-week's fishing for a crew. It is fortunate that the cod are sometimes so plentiful upon the ground that they can be caught without any bait at all. Then it is the fishermen use a double hook, cast in a mould, called a "gigger," the hooks being fixed back to back, with some lead run upon the shanks, in the shape of a fish. The gigger, being let down to the bottom, is played by sharp jerks, and many fish are enticed to it by its resemblance to themselves, and then, as Queen Cleopatra said, "they're hooked." This is a most laborious mode of fishing, however, as frequently the fish are hooked near the tail, when it requires a long pull and a strong pull to haul them on board.

The seine fishing being over, some thought is given to the fish in the stage. A day is generally devoted to them when all hands cannot go out fishing on account of the state of the weather, as, I may remark, we have our summer gales, the same as in other places. From the salt-bulk, some ten to fifteen tons of fish are thrown into a large vat filled with salt water, and washed thoroughly clean, and are then taken out and laid upon each other to drain. This pile is called a water-horse. Should the following morning be fine and clear, the water-horse is carried on hand-barrows, and placed, back downwards, on "flakes,"—that is, sets of beams which are supported on posts and shores—and covered with boughs. Much depends on the weather of the first two or three days; for should it rain on the water-horse, and continue raining for any time, the fish becomes of second or third quality, and only fit for the West India market. On the other hand, if two or three fine days are passed, your cod are pretty sure to turn out fit for the Roman Catholic markets of Europe. The fish having been "turned" each evening, about the third day they are put in faggots, about a dozen fish being laid one upon the other, their backs upwards, as a defence from wet or the dampness of the night. When sufficiently dry, a fine warm day is chosen to lay the fish out, singly, on a large stage; and during the hottest hours they are made up into a "fish pile,"—which is a large quantity of dry fish, built up in the form of a round haystack. When they are entirely cured — as they sometimes are—upon the flakes, they are still made up into a pile, in order to preserve them from wet, to give them a gentle heat, and to make room upon the flakes for others. The same routine follows with the remaining fish in the stage, and, "if fortune favours," a cargo of three to four thousand quintals of fish may be sent off to Italy in September.

As the reader may suppose, fish is, in Labrador, a standing—or, rather, the standard—dish. But although without cattle of any sort, we have a "compensation" of wild fowl of every description. But fowls — like hare — must be caught before being cooked; and during the summer months, Thursday was the day allotted to shooting. One or more of the masters in port generally accompanied the party,—if not to shoot, to cook for the rest. After rowing about eight to ten miles from the shore, we generally fell in with birds of all descriptions; those most easily obtained being the wild duck and goose. The latter is far superior to any of our tame geese in England, but is easily domesticated. After the day's sport we pitched our tent under a rock, made our pies, had our meal, and in short enjoyed ourselves mightily.

An incident, laughable enough in its way, occurred, on one of our excursions, to an elderly skipper who had volunteered to cook for us during our absence amongst the numerous small islands in search of the game. He had a great aversion to a gun, and talked vaguely and mysteriously of a "presentiment" that if he ever used one, some "dire mishap" would befall him, as it did that other ancient mariner. Arrived at our sporting ground, we left him to prepare our day's repast, for we never thought of eating more than once a day when out sporting; and then, I can assure you, we made an ample meal. On our departure, the skipper requested that a powder-horn might be left with him, in case his fire should burn low after his midday nap. He was a large and heavy man, and, like Mr. Wardle's fat boy, a great sleeper. His request for the powder was of course complied with; and away we started. On our return, late in the day, we heard, as we thought, the report of a gun; and on our joining him found that a "dire mishap" had indeed befallen him, but that without the use of fire-arms. The fact was, he had taken his nap, and—it is always so—had "slept rather longer than he expected," and finding the time for our return was approaching, and the fire nearly out, availed himself of the unfortunate horn, and shaken a few grains of powder on the heap of dry stuff he had placed on the dead embers, when, to his astonishment, this dry stuff formed a sort of train to the mouth of the horn, exploding the whole contents, and depriving him—narrow "shave"—of the whole of his whiskers and the greater part of his hair. After a good laugh at his expense, we showed him that after all it was of the powder more than of the gun, a man with a "presentiment" should beware.

The number of birds generally killed by three of us for the two days and a half amounted to about sixty. They were mostly ducks and geese; the proportion of the former, however, being ten times as great as that of the latter.

Besides the cod, Labrador is rich in salmon. The mode of catching these is with a "fleet" of three nets, which are fastened to each other so as to form a pourd; the fish in striking the first and even the second of these may not be meshed, but he cannot escape the third, as, when once there, it is impossible for it to retrace its swim. The mode of curing salmon is less difficult than that of curing the cod-fish. After being caught, it is merely cut down the back, cleaned, and put into puncheons, and salted and repacked in small casks for shipment. The mackerel also abounds in great quantities, with herrings, trout (of fine quality), and numerous other fish, all fit for the table, with the exception of the "lump" fish, which is nothing more nor less than a lump of blubber.

CHAPTER IV.

LIFE ON THE ISLAND.

In one of our weekly excursions we had a sharp chase after a deer, and killed him in the water, following him round a small island, and cutting off his retreat. After a great deal of trouble we made him take the water, and instinct directed him to the main land, where, had he reached it, he would have been lost to us. Immediately we found he had taken to the water, we manned our boat and away we went in chase. Although we had four good oars, he had got the start, and we could not overtake him, so we had recourse to the following expedient: when the deer arrived near the shore, one of our party fired a bullet direct towards the rocks where the animal would have landed, and the reverberation of the sound turned the animal towards us; and so, after a little dodging about, he became an easy prey.

The Labrador Fishing Establishment is also a general store, and when any one requires supplies the mode of dealing is entirely by barter. In a large establishment a special warehouse is generally fitted up—the ground-floor being generally devoted to hardware and groceries of all kinds; the second floor to drapery goods; the third floor to earthenware, boots, shoes, hats, caps, &c., &c.; and the fourth floor to blankets and rugs—both very useful, not to say absolutely necessary, in cold weather.

The mode of barter is as follows. A man comes to the office of the house, and delivers a "weight note" or a "quantity note"—the former for fish, the latter for oil. The price of this is filled in to his credit, and away he takes it to the warehouseman (who on the coast is a very independent sort of individual), and exchanges it for food. Such a system, I need scarcely say, is clumsy and inconvenient. Should the man want tea or sugar, he must buy a canvas frock, and convert the sleeves into bags in which to carry it; or should he have purchased stockings, they are equally useful for the same purpose; if rum is bought, it entails the additional purchase of a new tea-kettle (jars and bottles are rare and priceless).

In the summer season the hours indoors are very uncertain, although, of course, as much is made of the light time as possible. Early rising is the order of the day. Four o'clock is the recognised time, and, immediately on coming down, a dram of rum is taken by almost every person who can afford it. Flies and mosquitoes are troublesome at all hours, but less so in the early morning than when the sun becomes more ardent. Once we found an Irishman dead on the island, about ten miles from the Establishment, with his face half eaten away by these insects.

The mention of this poor fellow's fate reminds me that one thing we wanted on the Establishment was a surgeon, although, during my residence on the coast, we had (excepting the case to which I have just referred) only one death, and that from extreme old age. I am sorry to say drinking is a prevailing vice, and difficult to prevent, as, instead of beer-shops, as in England, we had floating hotels —where wines and spirits of all sorts could be procured—from Quebec and Halifax. On a free — somewhat over-free — coast like the Labrador, no license is required; you may sell what you like, and in any way you think proper. Under such a system intoxication is sure to be rife; still, what I may call the excesses of excess are not so apparent as the reader would imagine.

As the season advances, labour begins to slacken; still there is plenty of sport. The curlew has now made its appearance on the coast, and a most delicious bird it is, as every epicure must know. So bold are the curlews in Labrador, that you may sit on a rock at low-water, and, in the course of two or three hours, kill forty to fifty. These, however, make a heavy bag to carry, to say nothing of the rocky nature of the ground.

September is a glorious month on the coast. Then you may (as we often did) shoot the stag, and enjoy the pleasure of eating real Polar venison. A banquet of this is, to those who are necessarily compelled to eat so much fish, a treat more delectable than is the green fat of the turtle to an alderman. And here let me remark that, when a stag is caught, it is not stingily husbanded, but is dispensed with real good fellowship and freedom. Indeed, hospitality cannot be carried out with simpler grace or to a more liberal extent in any country than it is in Labrador. Every person receives a welcome on entering a house, and whatever the host may have you can share with him. And this not for a night only, but for a week if you desire it. The only compliment which passes from the visitor is, that he will be glad to "pay back, neighbour," when opportunity offers. In most ways the habits of the people are primitive. After the toil of the day, they will sit round a spacious room and crack jokes and make merry. On one occasion, I remember, matrimony was the topic ; and a youth who had been paying court to a young lass who had forsaken him for another swain, was bantered by one of the company on not being able to get a wife. The argument ran—as arguments on such intensely personal subjects sometimes do run—rather high, when the youth, to put an end to the whole matter, proposed the following terms, which he committed to paper, and got five of the party to sign. He bound himself under certain penalties to procure a wife in twenty-four hours from that time ; and they, in turn, bound themselves, should he fulfil his contract, to provide him with sundry household goods, the value of the whole being, perhaps, thirty pounds. The joke having taken this essentially practical form, the company separated, and away our Cœlebs went in search of a wife. I am rather sorry the prize was found so quickly, as one doesn't feel any great interest in such a story without the interest is prolonged. Within two hours, however, of his leaving the company, the blighted being was restored to happiness. He did not go to his old love, but accidentally meeting with a lass who had heard of the contract, and, strangely enough, fell in his way, she felicitated him in anticipation of his wedding, when he replied, "You shall be the bride, if you choose." The offer was coyly accepted, and the next morning they were man and wife—that is to say, as much man and wife as any pair can be beyond the reach of the rites of the Church. I hardly like to spoil the story by telling that he never got the furniture. The other parties to the contract slipped from their bargain, although the wife took very good care her husband should not slip from his. She was a bit of a termagant, and ruled him close, as if determined he should personally realise the wisdom of the proverb that "they who marry in haste, repent at leisure."

CHAPTER V.

BEARS—BLACK AND WHITE.

The white bear has one cub every year, but never deserts the first until it is two years old, when she has a third. Thus you may be sure when you see a she-bear, you'll find in the vicinity her two cubs. When—as has often been remarked, and as I frequently found during my sojourn in the North—driven by hunger, the bear is very bold and daring. They sometimes come prowling about the establishments, stealing what food they can, and making off without much haste or fear. The seal is its principal food. Although heavy in appearance, it looks majestic, and inspires something like awe as it sweeps silently over the snow. The white bear of Labrador may be termed the king of the frozen regions. Unless you have a quick eye and an unerring aim, my advice would be, should you meet one of these monsters, leave it alone. It happened, one fine bracing morning, I was strolling in search of game, when I came to a very difficult point or jag of land, which quite shut out from my view an inlet or cove which I knew was the resort of wild fowl. Finding it utterly impossible to round the point, I asked myself what I had better do. After a little consideration, I came to the conclusion to mount the adjacent cliff, go to the end of the cove, and, with gun in hand, cocked and primed, slide quietly down the slope, and be ready, the moment I reached the bottom, to fire on the game which I felt would be congregated on the spot. Imagine my horror when, on reaching the bottom, I saw, about ten yards from me, three white bears—an old she-bear and two cubs! What was I to do? I could not retreat without passing the monsters, and to attempt to pass them was like courting death. I waited patiently for the bears to approach. Resistance to the triad of monsters seemed useless, and yet, somehow, I resolved to die hard. I held my gun in hand ready for the first assault, and presently the old bear came slowly towards me, growling, but not appearing at all furious, or even in very great haste to make out what I was. Her all but calm way of peering at me as she moved leisurely along was even more terrible than I believe would have been her anger, and I lost nerve, and felt myself grow faint and half-oblivious. On came the bear, now silent as death. I stood like a thing inani mate; another measured step or two, and I knew she would be upon me—and yet I could not move. My eyes grew dizzy, my head swam round, and I can only recollect the monster's nose coming in contact with the muzzle of my gun, when, as if by instinct, I pulled the trigger, and down fell the monster at my feet! The report awakened me, for I found myself loading my gun (which I did in a short space of time), and took my place behind the bleeding carcase of the dead animal. The cubs did not appear to take much notice, but I was still in danger of the "two-year old," who presently made a move towards the dam, and, smelling the blood flowing from the death-wound in the head, set up a most piteous howl, then turned and looked me full in the face, as much as to say, "You are my mother's murderer!" I began again to grow frightened, but as the animal happened to turn towards the other cub, I again fired, and, as it was only a few paces distant and presented a fair mark, I literally blew its heart to pieces. To slay the third was comparatively easy work. The three carcases were laid together, and, without caring to shoot just then at smaller game, I walked off, thanking Providence for my deliverance. The weather coming on rough on the following day, and continuing so for some time, I regret to say I could not secure my prizes.

During this spring myself and a comrade had a most exciting race with a bear-cub in the water, but its rapid swimming and sudden diving bothered us a good deal. When alongside with it, we struck it on the skull with a hatchet, but it scarcely seemed to notice the blow, and certainly did not decrease the celerity of its movements. After about an hour and a-half's chase, however, we drove the cub on shore, and then very rapidly settled it.

The largest bear I ever saw could not have been less than fourteen feet long, and was stout in proportion. The skin would have made a comfortable carpet for a moderate-sized room. The circumference of the paws, which I measured, was twenty-five inches, and they appeared strong enough to crush an iron column.

The flesh of the bear is coarse and indigestible, and seldom eaten. One part of the beast is very useful, namely, the oil, which lies between the skin and flesh. This is highly prized on the coast as a liniment in cases of rheumatism. The skin of the beast, too, is of course more or less valuable according to size, quality, and colour.

The black bear is the most mischievous and

destructive animal with which the fisherman has to contend. It is fond of molasses, oil, and salmon, and some have been known to break open a store to satisfy their fancy in these directions. Old residents in Labrador have a great dread of seeing a black bear in the daytime, for the superstition is that its appearance forbodes a calamity to some person in the neighbourhood. Being one day in conversation with an old man who had resided on the coast fifty years, I asked him if he really believed the bear was anything more than a bear in daytime; upon which he became quite nervous, and, looking round him with doubt, as if a bear might be in sight and hear the callous way in which I spoke of it, he said—" Just you mind; it's no laughing matter, as p'r'aps this little story will show you!" I could scarcely repress a smile at the old man's earnestness of manner, but I listened attentively as he told me the following :—

"It is now ten years since I had an only son, a fine, strapping man o' thirty. He could do anything—save read and write—and do it well. He would have been a credit to the first Rifles in the world. Indeed," said the old man, with tears in his eyes, "I could speak about him all day, but I must tell you his story. There lived then, in Black Bear Bay, just to the nor'-west o' Seal Islands, a party of Esquimaux, and one day when my son was out deer-hunting he took refuge in the wigwam of the party from a passing storm. Two young Esquimaux girls were employed skinning young seals. Being of a goodnatured disposition, he naturally offered his services. Well, he remained there all night, and left the next morning, and came home. He never thought nothing of the girls—

how should he?—there was nothing very enticing about them to think of. It was not so with them; they had made up their minds to be his wives, and fancied they had only to ask to be accepted. So, without more ado, up comes the old squaw in a day or two, and took me all aback like with her request for my son. I knew he would not have them, and so I told the old girl. She mumbled some sort of threat on leaving my hut, and went home. Well, about a week afterwards, my son was out hunting with a gun up a salmon-stream, in a small boat, when what should he see peep out from behind a bush, in the broad daylight, but an enormous black bear, looking at him full in the face. He rowed towards the spot, and no sooner had he done so than the bear quickly vanished and appeared at another, and so dodged him until it led him to a fall (or small cataract) where the bear stood still boldly; but just as my son was on the point of firing, the beast again leapt away, and the boat went over the fall! My poor boy was picked up by a neighbour, shortly after the accident, but the shock was too much for him, and he died about two days afterwards. Before his death, he informed me in the most confident manner—and should I doubt a dying man?—that he was sure the bear was none else than the old squaw transformed. Now," asked he, triumphantly, "do you mean to ask if a black bear is no more than a bear?" I smiled, and asked myself the oft-repeated question, "Where are the missionaries?"

Throughout the depth of winter the black bear is in a dormant state within his cave—and yet not exactly so, for on opening his retreat and attacking it, it invariably shows some small amount of resistance. It makes nature its fortifier; that is to say, on the first appearance of snow it seeks the hollow of a rock, and there allows itself to be snowed in. To a practised eye, however, the place is easily discovered by the perforations on the surface of the snow, caused by the respiration of the brute; when it is found it is dug out and shot. Winter is the season when the animal is in prime order, and care is taken in slaying it to save the skin whole and clean. The oil, as I have said, is good for medicinal purposes; but, strange to say, I never saw it used for the hair. Indeed I was told that instead of nourishing the hair it burnt it off. What says Mr. Truefitt to this?

CHAPTER VI.

WOLVES, DEER, GAME, ETC.

The Labrador wolf fights well. He is cunning, but unlike most cunning things, he is courageous. He feeds chiefly on the elk and moose-deer, and, like the deer, he is gregarious. There are generally from eight to ten wolves in a pack. Their appearance is strange and striking in the extreme; they march just like the front rank of a company of soldiers, with their leader a little forward on the left; they keep about two feet apart, and when a herd of deer is sighted, at a given signal they break up into detached skirmishing order. In a short space of time, however, you will observe the whole of the skirmishers in a close circle round the deer, fast closing to the centre, when the conflict, being so unequal,—for the wolf is immeasurably stronger than the deer—soon terminates in the wolves sitting in banquet over the bodies of the conquered. The flesh of the wolf is worthless, but the skins are of value for drumheads.

On my paying a visit once to an old planter, I observed, suspended from the ceiling or roof of his hut by a small piece of cord, the skull of some animal. Being curious, I inquired if it was for use or ornament. " Bless me!" said he, "don't you know what that is? why, that is our weather-glass, barometer, and everything else; a wolf's head, and whenever we are on the point of having a change of wind, you may be sure that skull will indicate it, and what the change is to be." This made me still more curious, and I pressed him for more information. "I have had that skull thirty years," said he, "and—although a crafty wolf's—it never deceived me. Now look here! suppose the wind is north, and that skull's nose points to the east, and so remains for a week; after the wind shifts from north, we get an easterly wind for just as long as the skull pointed in that direction; and so on for any other quarter of the compass." He frankly told me he could not explain the reason, but so it was, and *so it is;* for I procured a skull and suspended it in a quiet place, and found, as the old man said, it never deceived me. I have since oft asked the question from old residents on the coast, if they could in any way give a reason for the weatherwise movements of the skull. One very naturally replied by asking me how I could account for the magnetic point of the compass turning always one way, and added that he thought the one just as mysterious as the other. "But perhaps," he said, "it's worth your considering that the wolf is always going head-to-wind in search of food, and as the wind changes so his course changes. Now is his instinct, as you call it, really in his skull?"

It is said of the wolf, and our domestic Labrador dog, that the breed is crossed, and that the Esquimaux dog is the result. During the whole period of my residence on the coast, I never knew or heard of any tangible proof of this; and I would rather favour the supposition that the Esquimaux dog partakes more of the fox than of the wolf: first, from its diminutive size; and secondly, from its fondness for all sorts of wild fowl and domestic poultry.

The deer has another most treacherous and powerful enemy, in the animal called the wolverine, or glutton, which is about the size of our common badger. On all parts of the coast are deer-parks or pasture-grounds, and also deer-paths leading to and from these pastures to a retreat in the wood. In many instances some part of the path is low from the proximity of the branches of the firs. The wolverine places himself on one of these low branches, and awaits the passing of the herd, when he makes a spring from his lair, and fixes his victim on the neck, and bleeds him until the deer drops, and becomes the common repast of the wolf and and other carnivorous animals abounding on the coast. On every hand the deer has his enemy, even the fox being sometimes marshalled against him. This antagonism, however, implies that the fox shall be very hungry and the deer very small.

Return we now to our fishing-home. While we have been wandering with the bear and the deer, quite a change on our small island! the ships have disappeared for their various destinations, and only a few unsuccessful fishermen are left to try and "fetch up lee-way" by exertion with the hook and line. What fish is thus caught is of the best quality, and is not landed, but kept on board ship in bulk, and taken to a southern clime for curing.

During my absence on my sporting tour, a rather romantic affair took place, which was related to me by a neighbour, but the truth of which,—absurdly improbable as the story seems—I can guarantee. An Irishman, named Glaveen, did not live on the best of terms with his better-half, and how to get rid of her in what he called a "dacent manner," was a puzzle, so he hit upon a most singular expedient. One fine morning, with much gravity marked on his countenance, he expressed himself thus: "Well, Biddy, I am tired of my life, and have been thinking about the other world, and how I could manage to do the thing in a quiet manner; now I will tell you my plan: I have heard hanging is about the most pleasant death a man could die of; and with your consent I mean to try it, only you stand by, and when you see me kick, you cut me down immediately." Well, poor silly thing! she agreed to what her husband had proposed. A rope was procured, a noose made, the same passed over a beam in the hut, adjusted round his neck, and hauled "taut," Pat himself standing on a stool the while. The signal being given, when the stool was removed and away, Glaveen kicked, and was immediately cut down by the unsuspecting wife. No sooner down than he exclaimed in a fit of transport and joy, "Oh, Biddy! sorry it is I am you cut me down; one of the most elegant deaths I was about to experience! The few moments I had in that state seemed a whole life to me; purgatory was passed, and behold, St. Peter, with the key of glory, came up to me and said, as if he knew me, 'Welcome, Glaveen, thrice welcome.' Then, Biddy, I thought of you, and should have been sorry to have left you without letting you know of my happiness; and how glorious it was to die by hanging. Now, Biddy, I will give you a chance: get up on the stool and try it yourself!" Sure enough the poor creature did as she was bid, and Mr. Glaveen, knocking the stool from under his wife's feet, left her swinging, but not to her fate; as one of the neighbours, who had listened to the whole affair, was immediately on the spot and cut her down just in time to save her life.

In September we generally had a visit from a Surrogate magistrate, in a schooner, but this is done away with; in fact it was a mere farce of a court. The judge was a retired post-captain in the navy, and the court was held on board a schooner hired for the purpose. It frequently happened that the judge got drunk, and then the scene in court was richer than anything in 'Pickwick.' As neither solicitors nor barristers came with the flying court, we had to manage our own suits. The only cases ever brought before the court were for wages. To give the reader some idea of this mode of justice, I may mention that a notice to the following effect was posted a week previously to the judge's arrival. "The Surrogate will hold a court in this harbour on Wednesday next, when plaintiffs and defendants may attend to try any case they may have to bring before the court." Wednesday arrives, and his Honour arrives as well, attended by clerk and sheriff's officer, for you must know the judge acted also as sheriff; and now the farce begins. The sheriff's officer acts as crier, and opens the court by proclamation, and all the early day there sits his Honour so consumedly drunk, as to be scarcely enabled to distinguish any of the parties about him; and after an hour or two's sitting, he abruptly settles all the cases, telling the crier to adjourn the court to the next harbour at ten the following morning; that harbour being, perhaps, twenty miles off. I was twice the victim of this "Shallow" justice; for on following the court to the next harbour for the purpose of getting an execution signed by his Honour, to my infinite disgust, just as I got alongside the schooner, I heard the orders given to "sheet home the topsail," and was politely informed over the bulwarks that the court had just adjourned to another harbour some twenty miles still farther on.

Such was the only court we had to deal with, and glad I was when I learned it was done away, for such a mockery of justice was calculated to bring both the British crown and the British flag into contempt.

We have indications now of the approach of winter. All life is taking a southerly direction, except ourselves who are compelled to winter on the coast. Flocks of ducks may now be seen continually flying south, and every day we have hints of what a lonely life we have to expect when winter really arrives. The days, too, begin to shorten.

Towards the end of October the books are closed and sent home to England for examination, duplicates being kept for reference. The last ship has gone from the coast, and we may fairly say we are cut off from communication with all parts of the world. Our nearest neighbours on the coast itself are ten miles off.

CHAPTER VII.

FUR ANIMALS AND SEALS.

BEFORE heavy frost sets in, we are busily engaged in trapping—chiefly for their furs—animals and birds of all kinds, such as the martin, the mink (a small amphibious creature of the otter species), the otter, the beaver, the fox, the wolf, the wolverine, the lynx or wild-cat, the musquash (a species of the rat), the porcupine, the hare, the rabbit, white and spruce partridges, and the ptarmigan. As the martin and the fox bear the richest furs, I will take them first. The martin, or what is termed in England the sable, belongs to a distinct class, perfectly pure in breed, but not very plentiful where I resided. The flesh is unfit for human food—indeed, the canine race will not touch it. Singularly enough, like the wolf, and, in fact, all wild animals on this coast, martins are always walking head to wind; thus an old hand told me one day, "Mark me, sir, if we have an easterly wind this fall, we shall have lots of furs." I asked him the reason, and he told me because the animals would in that case march towards us.

Of the fox there are several species on the coast, but the valuable breed known as "silver-hairs" are scarce. The "silver-hair" is the same size as our common fox, with a beautiful jet-black fur for the ground, which on each end is tagged with about an inch of "silver tinge," which glitters like jewels in the sun and snow.

When young, the "silver-hair" is easily caught, and becomes docile.

The next best foxes are the blue or slate-coloured, the patch or particoloured, and the yellow— the whole of which belong to one tribe, and form one family, as it is very common for a vixen to have a litter of five or six, and each of a different hue. The value of foxes varies much. The silver-haired and blue foxes would realise from twenty to thirty pounds each skin, while the patch and yellow would only fetch about one pound ten shillings.

There is another species of the fox on the coast, but almost worthless for fur. This animal turns white in the winter, and it is very difficult to see upon the snow. I once caught one alive, and tried to tame him like the others, but he was a sullen beast, refused all food, and actually starved himself to death.

The mink (of the otter species) is inferior in quality to the martin, the fur not being quite so long and bright, but in wear it is quite as durable; a good skin will pass muster with eleven martins'; the flesh is worthless.

The lynx, or wild mountain cat, is an extraordinary animal to meet; you would almost fancy, from his bold front, you were about encountering a tiger-cat; but on approaching to within about thirty yards, he generally turns tail and flies, when you can easily shoot him down. Although it is not cloven-footed, this animal is much esteemed as a delicate dish. Its size is double that of our domestic cat, but it has precisely the same form of countenance. The flesh is beautifully white, and partakes of the flavour of the hare; the bones are quite pearly, and are used by the Esquimaux for ornaments.

In some of the rivers the otter abounds, and is most destructive to the fishermen. The flesh is unpalatable, and the fur is used, like that of the beaver, by hatters. The mode of trapping the otter is exceedingly simple. Being of most cleanly habits, and liking to repose at early dawn (wild animals mostly feed at night) he selects a smooth spot on the bank of the river, which on the coast is called a "rubbing-place." This is found by the trapper, who is then sure of his game. The mode adopted is to bury the traps in the "rubbing place," and cover them lightly with the soil, particular care being taken not to disturb any part, but as near as ossible to keep the place as it is. On his visit the next morning, he is tolerably certain to be rewarded with a prize. The value of the skin of the otter is about two pounds sterling.

The musquash much resembles the common rat of England, and is found on the banks of the rivers; the skins are of small value, and are generally used by hatters.

The beaver of Labrador deserves special notice. It would almost appear to be endowed with reason, so remarkable are its habits, and so striking its ingenuity in the construction of its winter-quarters. With reference to the latter, the first step taken by the beaver is to find a pond and throw a dam across it, so as to retain water throughout the winter season. This done, a tree is selected and cut down by them, and falls in the direction they wish across the pond. The teeth of the beaver, I must observe, are curved inwards, are about a quarter of an inch wide, and some three-quarters of an inch long. Of course they vary according to the age. With these teeth they work, and on viewing the tree on which they have been engaged, you would fancy some fine carver had been at work with a sharp gouge. One thing, however, the poor beaver does which the carver does not do, and this betrays him to the natural foe of all living wild animals—man: *he leaves his chips* where they fall, and these point out his whereabouts under the ground. The beaver-house consists of three rooms or cells. The ground-floor is (to use an Hibernianism) in the water, the floor above is used for feeding, and the third as a sleeping-chamber. Most of the beaver-houses have an inlet and an outlet. If you find out the latter place, and stop it up, then you may consider the beavers your own. Having blocked the outlet, you dig and find out the inlet, which is generally near the bank of the pond, and under the water. There secure your traps, and in entering the dwelling or quitting it, they must walk in and be caught. The beaver is a social kind of animal, living in communities or families, generally consisting of five —father, mother, and three " papouses " (so the young beavers are called). Strange to say, you never see one without a companion (*Castor* and Pollux ?), and if you catch one, you are pretty sure in time to have the entire family. On the other hand, should they have been aware of your proximity to their habitation, the whole would have gone off and found a shelter in some neighbour's house. A small species of dog, called the Mountaineer dog, is very useful in directing the trapper to the beaver-houses.

The porcupine of Labrador is not in the least like its namesake of the East, the fur being a jet-black, with small white quills between the hairs. They are hunted for their flesh, which is considered a great delicacy by the inhabitants. They are generally found on the top bough of a large fir-tree. The small dog just mentioned is also employed on this errand, and immediately he comes where his instinct tells him there are porcupines he commences barking, and, on picking out the tree where an animal is located, he runs round and round the foot of the trunk, and continues his bark until the porcupine is bagged. This, however, is no easy task, for to really secure it you must cut down the tree, which may be fifty feet high. When the tree falls, the porcupine of course comes with it, when in dropping it generally makes a leap at either yourself or your dog, and, should it succeed in striking you, you don't soon forget it; for from its tail, which is its weapon, it discharges, as it gives the blow, a number of fine quills, which from their formation (being like the ear of barley) are so firmly imbedded in the flesh that to draw them is impossible, and you are compelled to let them work out of themselves the other side of the wound, wherever it may be. Fortunately the "quills upon the fretful porcupine" are not venomous, and the only pain is a rigid stiffness of the parts struck during the period the quills remain in the flesh. The porcupine's skin is of no value, but the quills are used by the Indians to decorate their mocassins or shoes. In size and shape the porcupine resembles the rabbit of England.

Gradually the winter creeps on, and the seal makes his appearance, also bound south. This is the last animal seen in the water, and great are the preparations for capturing it. A sealing crew consists of not less than six men. The seal-nets are carefully examined, and everything put in order before commencing operations. A fine, still morning is chosen to lay the nets down, which is cold but most exciting work. The net used is generally forty fathoms long and two deep. The foot of it is brought-to on a shallop's old rode, and the head on two fishing-lines with corks between. It is set to any depth of water not exceeding fifteen fathoms nor less than three, and is moored by a couple of killicks, fastened by eight or ten fathoms of rope to the ends of the foot-rope, which, by its weight, keeps the end of the net close to the bottom of the water, while the corks make it stand perpendicular. As the seals dive along near the bottom to fish, they strike into the net, and are entangled, for the net is placed with one end towards the shore, the other "right off." A long pole fastened to one corner of the net and a short one on the other corner (the former called a "pryor" and the latter a "bobber") show where the net is. The sealer lays hold of either, and by its means brings the head of the net to the boat. The crew then haul their boat along to the other end, and take the seals out as they go. Sometimes the nets are not seen until the frost sets in, when they are taken up through the ice, and the seals lifted out and drawn home on sledges. Should the water keep free from ice, the nets are visited every day and cleared. I have cleared as many as sixty seals out of one net.

The seal, from its very form and physical capabilities, becomes an easy prey to the fisher. Having the power to elongate or compress its body from the head to the shoulders, in striking the net it is elongated, but finding an obstruction, and perhaps fancying it has a foe to contend with, it compresses its neck, and of course tightens the mesh of the net and becomes strangled.

There is another method of catching the seal by what is called the stopper-net. Under this process one net is permanently fixed across a small channel—say between two islands—and another, called the entrance-stopper, is placed about one hundred yards to the north, one end being fastened to the opposite island and the other end attached to a long piece of rope in such a way as to allow the net to sink entirely out of sight. The end of this rope is made fast to a capstan, so as to be raised or lowered at pleasure. When a number of seals are seen between the two nets, the outer one is immediately hauled taut, and the seals, becoming aware of the fate awaiting them, examine every part of the net to find a hole large enough to escape from. Should they discover one, they are off through it (like a flock of sheep) one after the other; should they not succeed, they sometimes will attempt to cross the net overland, and are then easily captured.

CHAPTER VIII.

SEALS.

There are numerous kinds of seals, a brief description of some of which I will attempt to give. Of the few with which I have met, the largest is the Square Phripper. In season, it will yield about seventy gallons of oil. The skin is generally used for the manufacture of soles for boots. The length of this seal is from ten to twelve feet, and it is about six feet round. He is rarely caught in a net, being too wary. The only good mode of capture is with a gun. Even then, if the shot kills at once, and the animal is in water, you lose him: he sinks, and there's an end of your toil. If, on the other hand, you only wound him, he seeks the shore, and there dies. This seal furnishes, besides its valuable oil, a light airtight and watertight garment for the Esquimaux. The garment is made from the entrails, and weighs scarcely four ounces. As a rule, the Esquimaux are very clever in this description of tailoring. The dress is mostly well made, and is neatly and strongly sewn together with the inner lining of the windpipe of the animal. In fact all the thread used by the Esquimaux in the manufacture of boots, skin dresses, &c., comes from the same source.

The mode of preparation is simple. The windpipe is taken out, and the inner skin separated and dried; when dry it is cut into strips about two-eighths of an inch wide and about eight inches long. When these are required for use, the Esquimaux lady takes a bundle, and puts it in her mouth, and draws a thread as she wants it, as the operation of the jaw shredded the strips. With this, and nothing more, the Esquimaux works, but on the vellum the thread shows up beautifully white.

The next large seal met with on the coast is the Hooded seal, so called from the power it possesses of inflating an enormous hood over its head, containing about six gallons of air. Now these seals are not like their solitary brethren the Square Frippers, but are seen in large parties. Being on the ice, and meeting with a company of these animals one day, I had a good opportunity of watching their movements. On they came, though effectively to describe how would be a puzzle, as the seal, having no legs, moves with a spring and a half-leap. Their proceedings were saucy and independent in a degree.

On the strength of their hood (which you cannot hurt with a heavy club) they seemed to despise all fear. Their antics were really scornful, and appeared to tempt danger. It happened, however, that I and my party had provided ourselves with short muskets, and we despatched as many as we could conveniently carry off.

The mode of disposing of seals on the ice is first to kill them and then to take their pelts off. When this is done, and you think you have a sufficient load, you cut a hole on the top part of the skins, or pelts, pass a line through them, and drag them after you.

Next comes a seal smaller in size, called the Archangel. There is nothing peculiar in this animal except its name, and it may be passed over.

The principal seal of the coast is termed the

Voyage seal, while the males are distinctively called Harps, or Blackbacks. To mark a shoal of these animals, perhaps two or three hundred in number, quietly swimming, with head and part of the shoulders out of water—the head, by the way, being a jetty black, and the shoulders tinged with silver lustre—the coal-black eye shining at a distance like a diamond, is a magnificent sight indeed. I have often, I must own, felt remorse when killing these animals, there is such a human expressiveness in their eye, in fact in their entire visage.

When the first of these Voyage seals is caught on the coast a great sensation is the result, for this one, it appears, is the precursor of thousands, and a good "harvest" may be expected.

On one occasion I had charge of a boat's crew, and, on overhauling the nets, I heard the exclamation, "A Harp! a Harp, by George! Now, master," added the speaker, "we are going to have a rare voyage. Where is your knife?" The knife was soon found, and the tail of the animal cut close off to the body and carefully put away in the pocket for the following piece of amusement in the evening. On landing, the news soon spread throughout the establishment that a Harp had been caught, and the lucky skipper of the boat was complimented on his luck for securing it. Night came on, and the crews assembled as usual in their quarters. Not being exactly one of the crew, and living about two hundred yards away from them, I was politely waited upon by a lot of the old hands, and requested to attend on them forthwith, and to bring the seal's tail with me. I accordingly did so, and found the whole of the crews gathered together and shouting enthusiastically for "the tail." As I couldn't give it to all, I was requested by the senior skipper to nail it to a beam, where already figured a "tale" of fine dried tails of past years. I did as solicited, and, according to custom, I challenged any of the company present to remove the same without the use of his hands, which is tantamount to saying only with his teeth. Whoever tried and failed forfeited a quantity of rum, while the man who accomplished the task received a fine, to be dispensed for the benefit of all present, of two gallons of the spirit. In his turn he nailed up the tail, and when another succeeded in taking it down, the person nailing it up was again fined. So there was plenty of rum and plenty of merriment.

When the manager of an establishment finds a sufficient quantity of rum has been served to make the crew "comfortable" and merry, no more is sent them, and the Harp's tail becomes a memento of the evening, and is ranged amongst the other tails. This kind of seal produces about ten gallons of oil.

A younger seal than the Harp, but of the same species, named the Bedlamer, is also called a Voyage seal. It yields the same quantity of oil as the Harp, but the skin is not defined like that of the Harp. Once on coming on shore with a load of these animals we were met amongst the broken ice by no less a personage than a monstrous white bear, who, beset by hunger, and sniffing his savoury meat, swam boldly alongside, and, putting his huge paw on the gunwale of the boat, would have capsized her had it not been for the presence of mind of the skipper, who as quick as thought cut him across the paws, and compelled him to drop astern, although not before he had actually taken out one of the boat's thwarts, a plank eight feet long, ten inches wide, and three inches thick.

The next seal I have to catalogue (there is nothing special in it to describe) generally loiters on the coast later than the Harp, and frequents it sooner in the spring: it is called the Lazarus. The next kind is a small and beautiful animal, called the Ranger, which remains on the coast all the winter, and is sometimes found about the bays during the summer months. This species is very interesting, as they may be tamed and sent out fishing, which they will do readily. They are beautifully marked, and the skin is much esteemed by the natives. The flesh is sometimes eaten, but not often.

The "Jar" is a seal of social habits, like the beaver, living in large communities under the ice in winter, and in the numerous bays along the coast in summer. A remarkable incident connected with a search for this animal revealed to me a curious fact regarding the formation of the ice in the frozen regions. Being on a winter cruise for the "Jar," and night coming on without the likelihood of gaining shelter—moreover, not knowing exactly if we were on land or water, the snow being so deep—we built a snow hut, by cutting blocks of snow, and placing them one upon another, gradually inclining to the top centre. When nearly complete, there is a good-size square inside, and there we retired, and closed up for the night.

Now it happened, having found a small rise in the snow, we fancied we were on terra firma; but in this we were mistaken. We had located ourselves on the top of a Jar seal-house. One of our dogs gave the alarm, and fortunate it was he did, as doubtless before morning we should have all disappeared through the ice. We found however, there was no danger now we had warning, for beneath us there were three layers of ice. I inquired of an Esquimaux if such was always the case, and he answered me in the affirmative. I asked if it might not be the raftering of the ice. He said, No; raftering was very different.

Ice, as he explained, is said to rafter when, by being stopped in its passage, one piece is forced under another, until the uppermost one rises to a great height. I have seen the effect of ice-raftering on a small island near the coast. Many of the ice-rocks were placed in rows and circles much like the pillars of Stonehenge, only they were much larger and of greater magnitude. On visiting the island some year or two after, I found the character of the place quite changed. On inquiry, I was told, that in the previous fall a raftering of ice had taken place, and had broken the mass in fragments, entirely altering its appearance. It is a sad sight to see a ship on the weather edge of ice not enabled to work off; for when the ice begins to rafter she is thrown up, falls over, and becomes like corn between two millstones, and is literally ground up.

CHAPTER IX.

WINTER—CHRISTMAS.

"Now, boys, bear a hand!" cries the old skipper. Where are the dogs? Everything is getting fast, and we must have them whilst the weather is calm, or else we shall have a breeze springing up, and, mayhap, lose all our nets."

The morrow comes, and with it quite a new scene appears. The caulker has paid you a visit during the night, and when you wake in the morning and look around, — particularly towards the small patches of clear water in the vicinity of your island,—you will observe a vapour rising about four feet from the surface; and were you in the midst of it, you would not readily forget it. To use the expression of an old hand, "it cuts like a knife;" and sure enough it does. Nay, it rather acts like a furnace on the skin; for wherever it passes the bare flesh it burns the skin. You are now forced to wear a flannel mask on the face. In a few hours the whole surface of the landscape is one sheet of ice. Now comes a busy time — laborious, and in many instances dangerous in the extreme,—and you are actively employed in the operation of "cutting out your nets," which are generally placed about a mile off the shore. A watchman is kept on shore to indicate any change in the weather, and to keep his eye on the movement of the sea; for should a heavy swell suddenly break on the shore, it may shatter and scatter the ice, and you will then have to run for your life.

During one winter, it happened that a heavy sea broke on the shores of Labrador from the Atlantic, which pounded and then raftered the ice to a considerable height. The temperature then became mild for the time of year—December—the thermometer at about freezing point. With the change in the weather the seals made their appearance on the ice, which was so thick, and jammed or packed so tightly, that—once on—it was impossible for them to penetrate through to reach the water, and they thus became an easy prize. All hands but the cook were sent out to kill and pelt them. This continued for some days, which gave the men reckless confidence in pursuit of their game; and after repeated cautions from old hands not to stray too far from shore, in case of a shift of wind, two of the hands, disregarding the caution, went far beyond ordinary limits, and suffered serious injury for their temerity. There suddenly came a shift of wind, the ice moved, and the two over-brave—which is another term for foolhardy—fellows were taken out to sea. Fortunately for one of them he had on a pair of Esquimaux boots, but the other only had on mocassins, the uppers and soles of which are of the same material, and these scarcely covering up to the ankle. The Esquimaux boots are very differently made from these, and shield the leg right over the knee; and are generally so large as to admit of the wearer having on three thick flannel socks and a good large "boot-stocking" over these. Then comes the boot itself over all, tied above the knee. I leave the reader to conclude which of the two poor fellows had the best chance of being preserved from frost-burns. They both passed a wretched, dreary night, anticipating death with all the horrors of cold and starvation. The one with the boots could and did take exercise on the ice; but the other with the mocassins could not, his feet having become wet and stiff near the ankles. They drifted all through the night farther and farther to sea; but, fortunately, the next day the wind as suddenly veered as it had come, and late in the afternoon they were discovered not very far from the Establishment. They were soon rescued, and those rough men wept like children and fervently thanked God. I need not describe their appearance. They were placed in warm quarters, and the one who had boots on soon recovered. The usual remedy for frost-burns is—as the homœopathists will rejoice to learn—snow. A tub of this was procured in the present case, and the feet of the frost-bitten man were placed in it and rubbed to establish a free circulation, and to reanimate the burnt parts. This is done by rubbing with the palm of the hand. After they had rubbed some time, they drew off his stockings, when both feet came off with them, just at the ankle joints! There is no pain during the early stage of a frost bite, but merely a trifling sensation, as if a needle had slightly pricked you. The pain comes when reanimation and circulation take place; then it has all the arrowy agony of a severe burn. The poor sufferer, in the case I have described, being disabled for life, and there being no sort of sedentary employment on the coast, was sent to England, and being young, was, we subsequently heard, apprenticed to a tailor.

I must now return from the point where I diverged to relate that sad story, and describe the operation of cutting out nets from under the ice. A series of holes are made in a direct line over the nets, at about twenty feet apart, say for near half-a-mile. When this is done, two long poles, tied together, are put into the first hole, and, as it were, are threaded from one hole to the other. At one end of the poles is a line called a backing-line; and at the extreme end—say where the whole length of line has been passed under the ice—a creeper or small species of anchor is let down and trailed over the nets, which—when hooked by the creeper—are drawn up through one of the holes, the seals cleared, drawn to the Establishment, and placed in a heap which is covered with snow. Should the take of seals be great, this work continues for some days. When it is concluded, the work for the year is finished, and the crews quietly settle down, some in the backwoods and some on the coast. Those in the woods are employed either in cutting down timber or in building boats for the ensuing season, catching furs or deer-hunting, or in whatever hits their fancy best; but none are idle. On the coast the men are also variously employed : in mending salmon, herring, seal, and other nets, making new ones, and in many other employments. On every large establishment, for instance, there is a cooperage for the manufacture of casks to secure the oil rendered by the seal. At Christmas the men have eight days' holiday, when all sorts of rough sports are carried on. I say rough, because the forfeits, beginning with rum, invariably end in what is termed a "cobbing;" which means a dozen strokes across the soles of the feet with a wooden slice. Should any one of the crew absent himself from home on Christmas-eve, a deputation from the remainder is sent in search of him, and when found—even should he be enjoying himself at the big house or the cooperage—he is unceremoniously told to return to his home, and immediately he leaves the house the deputation commence chastising him across the shoulders with old shoes, until he reaches the dwelling where the crews are located, when he undergoes a trial for his desertion, and, as a matter of course, as it is Christmas-time, he is fined one or two gallons of rum. Very frequently more than one absent themselves, just for the sake of being fined, and to give more drink to the rest. The house these crews live in is fitted up in the dormitory exactly like a ship, with fifteen to twenty berths closed at the ends and open in the centre.

A favourite Christmas game amongst the men, enacted nearly every night during the holidays, is—or was—one called " Sir Samuel and his Man Samuel," in which you are to obey the orders of the first, but not of the second. Consequently, when Sir Samuel gives an order, his man contradicts it; and whoever obeys the latter becomes the object of "after-consideration," which means that he is physically punished, fined, or given some laborious task to perform. I have seen the last carried out, to the delight of many, on a lazy drone who was always skulking his work. His forfeit, however, nearly cost him his life. He was condemned to supply the room with six turns of wood; implying he should go to the stack of wood six times, which was at the foot of the hill, about three hundred yards off; and as he knew he would have no peace until his task was completed, away he went on his errand. I cannot well describe the night. The snow was dense in the air and thick on the ground, and the cold was bitter and biting. Moreover, on the day before, an extraordinarily large quantity of snow had fallen, and, from the extreme coldness of the atmosphere, it had become as fine as the sand on the coast of Africa, and as the wind came on to blow in the evening, it commenced drifting or flying in perfect whirlwinds. Only those who have witnessed a snow-drift in this form can conceive what it is like. It blinds and bewilders one, continually scudding round you, and making you white as the ground. Now this poor lazy fellow had made one trip with great difficulty, and proceeded on the next journey, but not returning quite so soon as it was thought that he ought to do, a lantern was procured, and on issuing from the house and seeing the state of the night, the practical jokers began to get alarmed. Although, as I have said, the pile of wood was only about three hundred yards distant, none dared go to it without a guide. This guide is not a living but an artificial one. A ball of twine is procured and one end made fast to the door-post and the other held in the hand of the "adventurer." One of the crew, with this guide, went to the pile, but when it was reached the missing man was not there. The whole of them then went with the same result. To attempt to trace him was out of the question; to halloo was useless, as the roar of the wind was awful. Fortunately the man himself caught a glimpse of the lantern, and made for it and returned home.

It is at Christmas-day that the old hands make their almanacs. I can best explain how this is done by giving the information as I received it: "Why, you see," said an old fellow, "I've got this 'ere board, and makes my almanac upon that. I divides the first day after Christmas into four parts, and takes notes of the quarter the wind blows from, and makes my observations on the same, and calls that January —each quarter o' the day representing a week; and I do the same up to the sixth of January, being twelve days after Christmas. I consider them there twelve days represents the twelve months of the year, and as I have made these almanacs for forty years and have always found them true, you can just laugh as much as you like." I must confess the owner of this almanac was always an authority as to how the summer would turn out, the time the coast would be clear of ice, what sort of fall it would be, &c. I visited the old man's quarters, and there I found, transferred from his board to the side of his room, sundry queer hieroglyphics which he said he understood well himself, and which I daresay he did. Coupled with the wolf's-head, this primitive way of rivalling Murphy somewhat impressed me : at all events, I have seen enough to know that only fools laugh at the simple lore of old folk.

CHAPTER X.

THE WOODS—WOOD-HOUSES, ETC.

TAKING advantage of a fine clear morn, I harnessed my team of fifteen dogs, and started up the Bay of St. Lewis to inspect the work that was doing in the woods, where the crews had been located in their habitations for near three months. Generally they settle down about two miles apart. Although dreary, cold, and in a sense out of the world, life passes with but few checks; for here, truly, man is monarch of all he surveys. He kills all he can, without certificate or fear of game-laws.

The settler, in fixing his home, selects a

square plot of growing trees, say about eighteen feet; he then cuts down the centre ones, and leaves the four corner ones, denuded of their branches to the height of about nine feet. On these four trees the "wall-plate" is laid, and upright timbers are placed side by side until the whole is enclosed, save a place for the doorway and the fireplace—the latter also answering the purpose of a window, as there are none in the sides of the house. The whole of the sides are caulked, or clinched, with a species of moss called on the coast "molldow." This caulking or filling-up the crevices makes the house all but air-tight. Next to the outer walls are the sleeping cabins, built precisely in the same manner as on board ship. The fireplace which, as I say, also admits light, is built inside, or square with the building, and is about nine feet long and four feet wide. The chimney being built entirely of wood, a "household engine"— that is, a bucket of water—is kept at hand, and a ladder kept stationed at the back in case of fire. It generally happens that the chimney catches fire two or three times a night, which, however, does not in anywise interfere with the sports of the evening. One pauses in his conversation, and quietly observes, " I say, Jack, the chimney is on fire; just take the bucket and cup, and sing out when you are up." Up goes Jack, and when on the top of the ladder he peers down on the company below, and sings out, " Here I am—look out!" and down comes the water. These small fires are so frequent that they are looked upon as matters of course, and the young grow up to manhood and teach their offspring how to manage them, but no one thinks of teaching them how to build a less dangerous description of chimney; but I have seen this dealing with *results* rather than with *causes* in far more advanced communities!

The roof of the house is composed of dried bark of the birch-tree placed on rafters. The bark is cut about three feet long, and from say eighteen to twenty-four inches wide. The floor of the house is composed of the same material as the sides—small trees cut and squared, and placed side by side. These are called "longers," which, I suppose, is an abbreviation for "long-layers." To live in the backwoods with a jolly set of men is a jolly life enough! There is no care; there are no taxes—no debts or duns; and there is ample occupation to keep the woodsman employed. One party of men are engaged cutting down trees for summer supply; others are felling them for various uses, such as the manufacture of staves for casks and shingles for covering roofs of houses. A wood-shingle,

I may explain, is a small piece of wood which answers the purpose of the slate in England. Another section of the crew are employed in the building of boats, and at one time the English Government gave a premium to settlers for building ships, but this is now a "matter of history." The premium, when it existed, was, that if a man built himself six ships, the English Government would fit out his seventh. I presume Government found the seventh was something special in size, and so the premium was discontinued.

The evenings in the backwoods are spent merrily enough; the nights being long, time must be passed somehow, and the woodsmen tell their stories, drink their rum, and sing their rough sea-choruses with the liveliest enjoyment. After supper there is generally a dance, the music of which (lacking ordinary instruments) is played upon the chin. The dancing is, of course, more gleesome than graceful, and both the male and female partners are somewhat desirous to shine in their movements. Now, should it happen that a traveller is passing your dwelling, he is sure to come in (without idle compliments passing) and share in the evening's festivities. Such is the hospitality of the country that everyone's house is open to everyone.

I forgot to mention one person who generally figures high in the woodman's crew—I mean the gunner, or the man who provides the crew with fresh craft—the term "fresh craft" signifying fresh provisions. I have already stated that all the fresh food you can get in the woods you must kill or snare ; and the gunner's occupation is to "develop" the rabbit-paths by setting traps. These paths are sometimes ten or even fifteen miles in length, and as many as seven or eight hundred rabbits will be killed by one man in the course of the winter.

Something rather ludicrous occurred during my sojourn in the woods. The reader must know that the men's axes should be very keen to cut and hew timber; and for the purpose of sharpening these tools, grinding-stones are kept by the crews. Now the climate is so severe, that cold water is not of the least use for the purpose of wetting the stone, as immediately it goes on it becomes ice. The only plan is to have boiling water. A crew I was visiting happened to be a double crew, two parties having built houses adjacent to each other; and one morning a man came to the "missus," and asked for a kettle of water, with which to grind his axe: "An' sure you can't have one, as it's full." "Well, then, let me have a boat's-kettle." "An' sure that's full." "Well," said the man, "if the kettle is full and the boat's-kettle is full, lend me one or the other of the saucepans." "An' sure you can't have any of them same—they are *all* full!" The poor fellow being disappointed, and not liking to be idle, went to the neighbour's house, and inquired if he could borrow a kettle or saucepan with which to assist him in grinding his axe. "An' sure," was the bland reply from another of Erin's daughters, "it's only just afore you came that Biddy borrowed the whole of my stock for something she was about indoors." Once more disappointed, he takes a sly peep into the hut, and there he sees Biddy literally up to her eyes in rice! The skipper had bought two bushels of rice in the fall of the year, and Biddy—not knowing the expanding properties of the grain—had put it all at once into a large saucepan, in order to give the crew a treat. Poor Biddy!

There she was—invoking all the saints in the calendar to give her help, as the rice boiled up and up, and came whitening over the pot; and by the time the husband came from his daily toil, Biddy had rice enough to last the two crews for some months. It was very laughable to hear the poor soul singing out to her daughter, 'Now, Nelly, fetch me another pan. Oh! Wishee!—wishee! The Deil's in the pot! Oh, Father, have mercy!—the blessed rice has multiplied, and is rising like a moniment up the chimney! Oh, run to the next house, and get me another pot, or a pan, or anything you can! Haste, Nelly—for this is getting worse than the widdy's cruse!"

CHAPTER XI.

THE ESQUIMAUX.

From the Bay of St. Lewis I took a stroll one breezy, bracing morning, towards the Esquimaux settlement or encampment, and was agreeably surprised at what I saw. I found them clean, and apparently cheerful. The wigwam they live in is built in a small valley, so that when it snows in the winter it will be entirely covered in. A plurality of wives was by no means uncommon with them; and, strange to say, I never heard of any disagreement amongst either male or female on that account. A denial is not known amongst them. The words "you shall not," and " I won't," are not in their vocabulary. Indeed I don't think their meaning could be explained to them. Some one in a family makes it known that he intends shooting deer on the morrow; another says, " I shall go;" another, " I shall stay here." Even the young ones, if they have a wish, are never denied its gratification; and so they live in unity and peace without anger or envy. How often do I look back on these people in their cold but happy home, where there is really no sin but polygamy! Theft is unknown, drunkenness is a stranger to them. In stature they differ less than any other people I know, the all but uniform height being about five feet six inches. They are capable of enduring much fatigue, are active in body, fleet on foot, and splendid shots to two or three hundred yards. While I was staying with them, one of the party, to prove his skill with the gun, performed the following feat:—As we were in the open country, and there was no tangible object to shoot at, he made a circle in the snow of about two feet in diameter, then stepping in the centre raised his gun perpendicular from the shoulder and fired in the air. After firing he stepped out of the ring, and in a few seconds, to my astonishment, the bullet came down within the circle he had made. He coolly remarked, "We want no targets to fire at;" and if a man can hold his musket with that precision as to cause the ball to return to fall just where he stands, what need has he of a butt? But the principal reason why they thus test their shooting is an economic one; not being always able to get bullets, they are chary of firing them away; and I have no doubt it is for the same reason that so many savage people have the "boomerang" or return-missile.

The Esquimaux are fond of music and dancing, are apt mechanics, and will readily imitate anything they see. For example, I showed one a violin, and on a visit to his wigwam some months after, I found he had manufactured an instrument from the birch-tree, the strings being made from the seal-gut. The most curious part was the bow. On asking him how he managed to make it, he pointed, with a smile, to his wife's head, and sure enough I found the hair on the head and that on the bow corresponded. The women, I should add, have long coarse black hair, kept remarkably clean, and generally plaited and strung with particoloured beads, which—like the modern hair-nets—have a pretty appearance. Not that the women themselves are pretty; nay, they are the very opposite, and appear all to belong to one family. Indeed so great is the resemblance one to another (and may not this arise, as with other simple people, from their common habits and customs—from their lack of individuality?) that it was some time before I could distinguish Tom from Jack. Like the settlers on the coast, they are very superstitious, and are easily worked upon. They have an extraordinary sight, seeing objects distinctly two or three miles distant, and telling if they are deer, or foxes, or what not. Another sense they have most keenly developed is that of smell. I have often travelled with them, and on seeing marks in the snow, they would immediately sniff it, and say what animal it was; and if it had passed within twelve hours, would say to an hour *when* it had passed; and— strangest of all—if the animal was in chase or being chased.

We get some fine sunshiny days on the coast in winter as well as in summer, and should the weather be calm, you may have an easy day's sport in the woods, and that without any expenditure of powder and shot. This is the mode you must adopt: Cut a stick some six feet long, at the end tie a piece of twine, with a noose or running knot; take your game-bag with you, and proceed to a grove of firs, examine the same, and amongst the lower branches you will see the spruce partridge, perfectly careless of your presence, airing himself in the sun. Walk noiselessly to the tree and place the noose near your victim, and with the grace and urbanity of a French criminal, he will quietly poke his head through and allow himself to be executed. The death is momentary, as the bird strangles himself; and as in so doing he makes no noise to disturb his companions, you may fill your bag in a short space of time.

The sport is very different if the wind blows;

the birds then are difficult to get at—the noose is useless—and it requires a practised shot to kill them properly, as if struck anywhere else than through the head, they are not eatable; tasting bitter as the spruce. These partridges do not turn white in winter. They are much like the grouse of this country, and are quite as good eating when properly shot. The white partridge is, as regards habits and food, the reverse of the former; and affords at all times exciting sport. After a heavy fall of light snow, say to the depth of six or eight feet, if the weather be calm and the sun bright, you may observe numbers of these delicious birds disporting themselves *in the snow.* I say in the snow, as from the intense cold and fineness of its quality, they take a dive in it some eighteen inches under the surface, as if it were water, and rise eight or ten feet from their starting point. This it is which makes the sport exciting, as when the bird dives, he is just as likely to take a right as a left angle, or to go straight ahead as to take either; and you have to be quick, both of eye and trigger, to hit him at the very moment he reappears. These birds feed on the buds of the birch-tree, which give them a peculiarly fine flavour; indeed the crop of the white partridge, when it is cut open, affords quite a "bouquet."

In extreme severe winters the Esquimaux—from whom the partridges led me—are often hard driven for food; then the toil to procure it sometimes results in the death of the hunter, or "watcher." Here is a touching instance in illustration. Let me, however, premise by saying, the seals which are not migratory may be found all through the winter in the different small bays, and may be caught by stratagem and patience. In a former chapter I have said that this animal, like the beaver, is of social habits, and lives in communities. But one thing is essential for the life of the larger sort, and that is a constant supply of fresh air. For the purpose of obtaining this necessary element, holes are kept open by the seals throughout the winter, and are called by the Esquimaux "blowing-holes."

On a fine cold day you may see the seal basking in the sun near his hole with perhaps one or two Esquimaux warily watching his movements; for should the seal hear the slightest noise, down he goes to the waters beneath. But should the surface of the hole have become frozen during the afternoon's nap, he has no time to open it before his pursuer is upon him, and then he becomes an easy prize. The mode the seal adopts when he discovers he is frozen out of his element is curious in the extreme. Finding himself disturbed and the means of retreat cut off, he stands as it were on his head, and, using the fore-fins or phrippers as a motive power, whirls himself round at an inconceivable speed. The mouth being open during the rotary motion, acts somehow as an immense auger, and soon penetrates the five·or six inches of new-formed ice on the surface of the blowing-hole.

Now—coming to my narrative—it happened that an Esquimaux family were hard pressed for food, and for some time the weather was so boisterous that none dared move out. Fortunately a lull came, and with it sunshine, and then away went the watchers to examine the blow-holes in the bay, in the hopes of returning in the evening with a prize. On these excursions the watchers are provided with a small stool to sit on. Besides this they have a sharp spear, made of bone, arrow-shaped, and inserted in the top of a stave about four to six feet long. Attached to the spear is a long cord, manufactured from the skin of the seal. The end is generally made fast, if on land, round the body of the hunter, and if on the water, to the kyack, or canoe.

Now it chanced that one of these watchers, a woman, had observed a monster seal for some hours; and, feeling assured the hole had frozen so that she could reach the spot before the seal could bore through the ice, she ran forward, dart in hand; but, observing her movements, the animal was on his head in a moment and turning round like a spin-top. The poor Esquimaux hastened up and plunged the dart through the seal's skin, but unfortunately he had just finished boring, and down he went, with the dart firmly fixed in his hide. The act was so sudden the poor creature had no time to disengage the cord round her waist, and was drawn across the hole with such frightful force that she was doubled up as it were in a funnel, without the power of moving, the seal acting as a dead weight on her body. When her companions came up, they had the sickening sight of beholding her broken corpse, attached to which was the monster seal, still plunging for liberty. After much toil they disentangled the corpse, and killed the animal,— a sorry recompense for the loss of a sister.

Such are some of the hardships these poor people undergo. The youngest are sent out trapping or catching furs, and begin a hard hand-to-hand battle of life when other children are just sent to school.

The burial of the Esquimaux is an interesting

ceremony. A heap of stones is gathered; the "kyack," and all the departed's hunting implements, are collected and arranged in order by his side, with a supply of food, a pipe, tobacco, &c. When the preparations are complete, he is taken to the pile, everything is placed in order around him, and then all is carefully covered over to the height of about four feet, apertures being left here and there to admit air. The grief of his friends is calm but touching. The Esquimaux, like the Greenlanders, believe in the immortality of the soul, and that the dead go to the land of spirits, and there enjoy the felicity of hunting from age to age, while the body remains behind and moulders in the dust.

The women have seldom more than two or three children, and these at the intervals of two or three years. They are very fond of their offspring, and carry them in a hood on their back wherever they go, suckling them for two or three years. These children are quiet, and, as I have said, never know a denial. They are brought up without fear, and, I may remark, without vice.

The people are very jealous of the resting-places of their departed relatives, and make frequent visits to them to see if the tomb has been disturbed. Whenever they find it has, great is their tribulation, as they consider some dire mishap is about to fall on the family. I know of more than one Englishman who visited some tombs, and finding only the blanched bones, took two or three skulls away, much to the terror of the Esquimaux, who, I believe, could they have identified the culprits, would have slaughtered them on the spot. Strange to say, during my sojourn on the coast I rarely heard of any sickness among these people. Neither insanity nor idiocy is known. The women live to a greater age than the men, the latter generally dying at the age of from fifty to sixty, and the former at from seventy to eighty.

The Loon, a large fowl of the diving class, furnishes them with covering instead of blankets: the skins are dried and sewn together, and are impervious to wet. In fact the whole of the clothing made by these people has this same quality. As fashion is not studied, a suit of clothes or a cassock and trousers are supposed to last ten or fifteen years. The dress of the female much resembles that of the male, only it is more elongated in the back.

In winter their principal food is the seal, which is sometimes eaten raw. They are also fond of the oil as a sauce for other dainties, amongst which are the entrails of the deer. This boiled with seal or train oil is a favourite dish with them. Truly, there is no accounting for tastes!

CHAPTER XII.

ADVENTURES—FOX-TRAPPING.

I REMEMBER that on returning from my visit to the Esquimaux encampment, I found, on reaching the landwash, where I and my party intended to cross to our station, the sea heaving in from the broad Atlantic. It was a strange sight—the ice rolling like the waves of the sea, but still too thick and tough to be broken. It withstood the force of the under-rolling waves that night. The dog appears endowed with a keener sense of danger than man, for on urging ours—to the number of fourteen—to take the ice, they one and all lay down and refused to move. Of course we had the sense to be guided by them, and return along the shore to a narrower part of the bay, so as to cross in safety. After some difficulty, and a walk of ten miles, we reached the mainland, and found shelter for the night in a woodman's hut. Early in the morning I started alone, leaving my man and dogs to come after me, following my track through the snow. I had gone about five miles, when crossing the river-head, or extreme end of a small cove, I found the sea had increased in violence, and the ice had commenced breaking adrift; with some risk I crossed to the opposite side, when on looking towards the point from which I had started, I found there was a space of some feet of clear water, with the sea already breaking over the beach. Communication I knew was now cut off from the dogs in that direction, and they would have to make a circuit of at least ten miles before they could reach me. About mid-day I lost sight of the sun, and, to my consternation, it began blowing, while the breeze was accompanied with a regular snow-storm and drift. To have remained stationary would have been death. Every now and then I looked at my compass to direct me to an island about a mile distant from the one on which I resided; and, thanks to Providence! I reached it just before dark. I then made an attempt to cross to my own island, but it was only a faint effort, as immediately I ventured on an ice-pan a sea hove in and sent me and the pan about five feet on the rocks.

The island I was on was inhabited in the summer months by fishermen who migrated from Newfoundland to prosecute the cod-fishery, and returned in the fall to their homes to sell their hard earning for cash to the Spaniards and others who resort there for the purpose of purchasing for their own markets. True the houses of these fishermen, from the primitive way in which they were built, afforded but little shelter, being, for the most part, unroofed. But necessity is the mother of invention (as I have found perhaps as frequently as the reader has heard), and, knowing all the huts well, I selected the best—though bad was the best—and set to work to make it habitable. The roof had fallen in with the weight of snow, but in a neighbouring stage or shed for curing fish I found a quantity of dry spruce-boughs, with several empty casks of large dimensions, with one head out. I made a bed in one of these with the boughs, and placed the closed head to windward, and thought I was about to sleep, imagining the sledge and dogs would soon overtake me. I must inform the reader that when in the morning I had quitted my companions, I had left everything behind me, even my matchbox, gunpowder, tobacco, and drinking-flask. Into the kennel I had prepared I now crawled, but I soon found my blood begin to chill, while a pressing sensation came across my temples, with a coldness across my chest. Fortunately I knew the remedy for the latter, which was to tighten my belt; and so, as soon as I found the pain begin, I drew the belt tighter and tighter around me. Fortunately I had a good fur cap, but from the fatigue of the day, and from having perspired freely, it became cold and made me feel uneasy. I knew now if I slept I should never awake. Luckily for me I had two pocket-handkerchiefs, one silk and the other cotton. I took my cap off, and tied the cotton one over my head and face, and then I bound the silk one over it. This, I have no doubt, saved my life. My time was employed the whole night in walking backward and forward, and every now and then I found myself striking at some object, which I fancied had entered the shed, when, my fist coming in contact with a cask or post, I was suddenly called back to consciousness. Thus I passed fourteen long and dreary hours, and when day broke it was beautiful bright weather, with the thermometer at fifteen to twenty degrees below zero! As I felt hungry I again tightened my belt and felt relieved. I visited the spot where I attempted to cross the night before, and found the ice all gone, and the sea smooth as glass to the opposite island, a distance of about three quarters of a mile. The wind, having shifted in the night to the north-west, had sent the sea down, but had brought intense cold. To have attempted to retrace my steps from where I started the day before would have been madness, as I could not have borne the cutting blast. I said to myself, "The ravens are now plentiful on the coast, and——," and then I prayed to the Father of all. About noon I fancied I heard the bark of dogs, and, on going on a rise of the island, I had the great joy of seeing the whole team bounding like mad things, about a quarter of a mile off. Soon they gained up to me, and I asked my man for something to eat and drink. "Lor bless your soul, sir," was his reply, "we have been out all night in the bush, only we had a fire, and all I have are a couple of biscuits and a drop of rum in the bottle, which you must not yet touch."

The first thing we now did was to kindle a fire, by knocking one house down for firewood. After boiling some water, I had a small drink of rum with some water and part of a biscuit. Having now my tobacco, a good fire, and a companion, the night (although I was still all but in the open air), was not so dreary as the last. On the morning of the third day we proceeded to the landwash to see if the ice would bear. The dogs refused to cross, and we were compelled to remain until afternoon, when they crossed without fear, and—although the whole journey was but ten miles—we arrived at home about four o'clock of the third day of our starting. Our friends anticipated what had happened, and had everything prepared for our reception. On my nearing the Establishment I was met by two of the old hands, who congratulated me on my narrow escape, and tendered cautions touching the danger of eating too much at first, which, they assured me, might bring on inflammation. I took their advice, and profited by it, as I never suffered the least inconvenience from my night in the snow; and, moreover, it taught me never again to travel alone in a wild and dreary country. After my long fasting I was never better in my life, and on the third day I felt as if I could have walked any distance without feeling fatigued. When the Esquimaux are pinched with hunger, they adopt the expedient of bracing themselves every time they feel it coming on, and I am told they will live many days with only a small quantity of food and a little drink. From abstinence the Esquimaux hardly know any of the ills which flesh is heir to in our over-feeding civilized communities. The only complaint they suffer from is blindness at an advanced age in the left eye; the females are especial victims to this affliction. I don't recollect meeting one over sixty years of age who had not lost the sight of the left eye. This prevalence of blindness doubtless arises from the glare of the sun on the ice in the spring of the year, when millions of discs are formed in a single focus to the eye; the effect is, that the "beholder" becomes suddenly blind for some days. The remedy applied is simple, but especially painful: a tub of snow is procured and the patient has his or her head enveloped in a hood, which falls down and reaches round the edge of the tub. A shot is then made white hot and thrown into the snow; instantly a cloud of steam is engendered, the film before the eye (caused by the action of the snow) bursts, the humour is scaldingly discharged, and the sufferer receives immediate relief. Of course the patient is kept in a dark room for some days, so that the tone of the nerve may be re-established.

Shortly after my return home I began to devote myself to my fox-traps. It is a hard employment, but exciting and healthy. Some fine morning away you trudge with half-a-dozen large iron fox-traps on your gun, across some five or six miles of the most barren part of the island, and these you set on the land, elevated so that they shall not be covered in with the snow—each about one mile apart from the next. Great care must be taken in setting them so as to disguise the place, which must look as if no traps were there. Two holes are cut diagonally with each other, and in each of these you place a trap (having first tied the bait under it), and neatly cover it over. In this you cannot be too careful, as if the fox saw the least sign of iron he would know it was "unnatural" to the place, and leave it alone. Sometimes a fox will dig in the immediate neighbourhood of a trap, with the hopes of undermining it, but in this operation—clever and characteristic as it is—he is generally caught by the under-jaw. One day I found a fox in this situation quite alive, having but just been trapped. He had displayed great cunning in his mining operations, but just as he thought he was about walking off with his prize, "click" went the spring, and he was captured.

The skin of the fox being more or less valuable, care is taken in killing him so that it shall be injured as little as may be. The common practice is to throw yourself across the body, seize him by the throat, and press the knee on his chest; and then, when you find the heart cease to beat, to strip poor Reynard at your leisure. This smothering process keeps the skin free from blood, the stains of which would lessen its value. Besides the fox, chance may throw a martin in your trap, or it may be a weasel—the rich ermine of which is rather scarce on the coast.

After these daily excursions, the evenings are

generally spent in some cheerful way—mostly in telling stories of home and youth, as if to refresh the bleak Present with a peep of the ever-roseate Past.

CHAPTER XIII.

SPRING, SPRING-DUCKS, ETC.

It frequently happens on the coast that in midwinter we have what is termed a "silver-thaw," when it rains and freezes at the same time. The wind is then generally from the east, the weather is boisterous, and numbers of birds of two kinds—the one kind lean and the other fat and well-favoured—come whirring down upon us. The former is the ptarmigan, a bird of the grouse kind. It generally weighs about a pound —seldom, if ever, more. After the long journey these ptarmigans must have had, they arrive in poor condition, and are scarce worth the trouble of killing. It is not so with the other sort—a delicious, small but plump bird, called on the coast the "snow-bird," and in England the ortolan. Of these I have caught as many as two hundred a day. They are, even in Labrador, one perfect mass of fat, but are not of an over-rich flavour. They are, as in England, about the size of our bullfinches, and I have had as many as a hundred in a pie at one time, which beats the "four-and-twenty blackbirds."

These birds are always the forerunners—generally, in one sense, the bringers—of rough, stormy weather, when the seals again make their appearance, and when some fresh sport is unexpectedly afforded to those who are fond of it. With an easterly wind the weather is generally thick, and the sun is obscured. The temperature, too, undergoes very rapid changes: at midday it will thaw and in the evening freeze, so that the ground becomes dangerous to walk on. We generally wear what on the coast are called "creepers," which are made in the shape of a cross with thick "starts," and which are much the same as cricketers wear in England. Many a fall have I had over a rock during the prevalence of a "silver-thaw," and only had Providence and the creepers to thank that I have not been seriously injured. After the thaw, bright sunshine appears again, with a cold, cutting, north-west wind, "bracing up the nerves," as the fishermen phrase it, "to the tune of 'No Doctor Wanted.'" Plenty of exercise, an ample supply of good plain food, and an all but *raw*-edged appetite, keep the medicine-chest well closed. The only time during my residence that I was particular, even as regarded extra clothing, was in the spring of the year, when the ice began thawing. Then I took to flannel, which, as summer came on, was left off, and the ordinary skin-dress resumed.

The spring of the year—which the reader will be kind enough to imagine has dawned upon the coast—brings on a busy time. The pounds in which the seals caught in the fall of last year were placed, are opened and exposed to the heat of the midday sun, so that the skin may be thawed from the fat of the animal. When sufficiently thawed, skinning takes place, and the most expert and strong-armed men are employed for the purpose. Under favourable circumstances, one man will take off about fifteen skins a day. The fat is then removed and placed in a store for the purpose of being cut up into small pieces, so as to be easily melted and converted into seal-oil. The operation is thus performed: a man takes what is termed a "rand," or large piece of fat, just as it happens to be cut off the animal, and, placing it on a table, sticks a steel behind the knife, and cuts away in the same manner as is done in England when suet is cut up for a pudding. When this is done, the process of what is termed "rendering out" the oil is commenced. On large establishments, from four to six or eight large iron boilers are erected in brickwork; and in these the fat is placed, the fires are lighted, and, when the whole boils up, the manufacture is complete. Great pains must be taken not to allow the mass to boil too much, as over-boiling decreases and discolours the oil. When properly "done," the oil should be of a pale straw-colour. Many a savoury dish is cooked in this boiling oil. One—a great favourite with the settlers—is the same as that cooked on board the South Sea whalers, and known as the "South Sea tea-cake." Here is the recipe: take of flour and water enough to bind the former in a stiff paste, then consolidate it into the consistency of dough with brown sugar; when this is done, roll it out into thin pieces, like wafers, and cut according to your taste. Throw the pieces on the boiling oil, and they immediately swell up like an egg; and, except that there is no egg in the business, are much like the cakes made in the island of Jersey, called "merveilles."

After taking out as much oil as possible, and placing it in a tank, the remainder in the boiler, called "scrunchens," is collected, and undergoes the process of being pressed with a strong screw, just as tallow-chandlers press the fat after the sundry substances collected by them, from which to manufacture candles, have been melted down. When sufficiently cool, the oil is placed in casks for early shipment to England in the summer, or, should a quantity have been "caught," a ship is at once despatched with the cargo. Talking of ships, I may briefly mention—and throughout, let me parenthetically add, I have studiously cultivated brevity—that, during my residence in Labrador, I "commanded" a schooner of forty tons; and although a young navigator, I cannot help feeling proud when I remember that for five years I skirted the coast without a casualty. I could cull some adventures from my "Log," but none of them sufficiently special or interesting to be chronicled.

Collecting the oil in the spring-time is a pleasant occupation, and affords fine opportunities for viewing the constant changes but perennial loveliness of Nature. The frozen tide thaws and twinkles in the sun, the snow gradually disappears, and here and there a green streak of vegetation may be marked; and soon the beautiful wild waterfowl dot the water.

The bird called the Hound—a graceful fowl, rather larger than a teal—is very abundant. These birds migrate to the north in large flocks in the spring, and as they fly make a continual noise, than which nothing can more resemble the cry of a pack of beagles when in chase. When and how they return south is not known for certain. They make pretty points in the landscape, and eat well in a pie.

The mornings, now that spring is breaking, are for the most part fine and clear, with a perfect Italian sky. Not a cloud is to be seen; all is beautiful and blue and bright. Now begins the slaughter of the ducks going northward. At early dawn about the middle of May four or five men repair to some small island near the mainland, and there erect what is termed a Gaze, which is like a small fort cut out of the solid ice close to the landwash. Immediately the ice clears off the coast, only for twenty or thirty feet, clouds of ducks wend their way from the south to breed amongst the numerous islands on the coast; and these are popped at from the gaze as they pass the point of land.

We consider it a poor morning's work if we do not kill (say for four guns) at least one hundred to one hundred and twenty ducks. The shooting begins very early, and generally ends about ten in the morning, when we amuse ourselves chasing the crippled birds, which is more exciting sport than may be at first imagined. The punt loaded with our game, homeward we hie for breakfast; and a jolly meal it is, the allowance being a duck a man. We do not take the trouble to roast them, but, cutting them up in joints, we fry them; the livers, gizzards, and hearts being served up afterwards as an extra dish. Then we take copious draughts of drink, christened on the coast "callibogus,"—a mixture of rum and spruce-beer, "more of the former and less of the latter,"—when the meal is over. Those employed in killing the birds assist the cook in divesting them of their feathers, which is done in the expeditious manner which I have previously noticed. The time allowed is a minute a duck. The wing and tail feathers are, to describe the process in full, first drawn, and a large iron boiler being placed on the fire, and the water made steaming hot, and kept so, one duck after another is thrust therein, and is just sufficiently scalded to admit of the feathers being rubbed off in a mass. The ducks, having been unfledged, are packed away in casks, and salted for summer use. The feathers are dried, and sometimes sent home; but not often. Yet such is the closeness of the feathers on the eider duck that it only takes seven birds for one pound of feathers. The duck-shooting lasts until the middle of June, and it would be difficult to compute the large number of birds which are killed in that period. The weight of one of them is, without the feathers and when full grown, about five pounds. The gun employed for their destruction is of large dimensions, and, being used as a shoulder-gun, punishes the sportsman fearfully. After a good morning's work, when the birds seemed in a hurry and whizzed past quickly, I have been so bruised in the shoulder as to require a pad stuffed with feathers before I could venture to fire the first gun the next day; but immediately the sport became exciting the pad was thrown away, and all pain seemed for the time to cease.

In the middle of the day the birds take their meal on the shoals in the neighbourhood of the small islands. Consequently during the time of their repast we are idle, and take a walk to some hill, where we crane our necks and strain our eyes seaward, trying if we can spy any sail in sight from Old England. How many false visions appear! One of the most remarkable phenomena of the coast is the mirage, or fog-loom, when objects take monstrous sizes, and when mere cockboats expand to three-deckers! You see a ship with her spars towering, as it were, high into the air, but gradually, as she breaks through the bank of fog, she dwindles down to a small craft of some twenty or five-and-twenty tons! Mock-suns are very common on the coast. I have seen as many as three of these luminaries shining at once. This mostly happens in winter, just on a change of weather.

Returning from one of my duck-shooting excursions, I was informed that our stock of flour was nearly all destroyed by the rats, which, always numerous and troublesome on the coast, had eaten into no less than six barrels. In some they were so plentiful that they caused the casks to move.

Rats are a perfect pest in Labrador. They eat up our food (fortunately, on the occasion I have mentioned, there was no fear of famine, as it was in the spring of the year), and they seem to delight in destroying the fishermen's nets. They are very prolific, and I myself have counted no less than seventeen in one net. The dogs are trained to kill them, and a premium of a small portion of rum is given to the men for every rat killed, which on large establishments amounts to something considerable. In the course of a year I have had tallied, or counted, as many as seven hundred, which cost for killing nearly twenty-two gallons of rum. The same rat cannot be brought a second time for the premium, as on being produced at the store the tail is cut off and destroyed.

The whole routine of last year is now carried on. I should like to describe the breaking up of the ice, but it is beyond my power. In the different bays are brooks, and in these brooks are "rattles," as they are termed, or, more properly speaking, "falls," though none are of any great magnitude. The nearest to our establishment was ten miles off; and as the thaw came on in the spring, which of course swelled the brook, great curiosity was manifested by many as to the time the fall would burst or blow up from the pressure behind.

Although but small, it had its influence on the bay. It was about twenty feet high by some forty feet wide, and on its bursting set the whole of the bay ice free. It is impossible for the pen to convey any adequate notion of the bursting of this fall. Think of some tens of thousands of tons of water pent up behind a barrier of ice some twelve to fourteen feet thick, and think of the whole mass bursting through in an instant! The loudest thunder is light by comparison. Then comes the confusion, the mad whirl of water, the swelling and roar of the brook as a hundred small and rapid streams are melted, and pour into its one common channel. For days the noise is deafening, and the boldest men grow strangely nervous. Every one now has to work hard. If you have built your house too near the sea-shore, it is just as likely you may find the habitation moving seawards like a Noah's Ark. Large rafts of timber may be seen floating off in the same direction; in fact when the ice moves it bears off everything which is upon it. The rush of water from the brook brings down masses of earth with trees still in them, and these, too, go floating away upon the ice. Everything moves in one calm, seemingly resistless manner and direction.

The bay once clear, the woodman returns to the coast to resume his summer toil. A few are left for a week or two longer to procure the rinds, or bark of trees. Their work is called "rinding." One length only of bark of about six feet is taken off the lower part of the trunk of the tree. The chief use of rinds is to cover the roofs of houses and the piles of fish.

It is now, as the spring literally "bursts" upon us, that retreating winter shows us his victims. Let me give an illustration. Some one has been out shooting, and he returns with the melancholy news that a poor fellow has been found dead and frozen under a cliff. It is the corpse of some one who had wandered from home in the winter, lost himself, been overtaken by a snowdrift, and perished from cold and starvation. I was generally requested to read the Burial Service over these remains, which, as there was no clergyman at hand, I could not refuse to do.

One of the pleasantest sports of this season is exploring the island for eggs and eider-down. The eider-duck makes a rough nest on the ground, generally between two rocks, and deposits four to five eggs, sometimes more. An island being selected where they are known to resort in large numbers, it is reached at nightfall; the nests are visited, eggs destroyed, and the down taken away. We then retire to the leeside, and remain the night. On the morrow we again visit the nests, and find them newly lined and a new-laid egg in each nest. This visit generally satisfies us, as from the quantity of birds on such an island we are enabled to collect a thousand or more eggs and an immense quantity of down.

CHAPTER XIV.

FOXES—TALES— SEA—TRACKS.

SHOULD all the foxes not have migrated from the islands to the main land, your sport for eggs and birds on such islands will be barren of results, as they destroy the former and catch the latter. The capture is easy enough, as the duck sits very close, and can even be caught by hand if you go "down wind" on them. In visiting my fox-traps in the winter I frequently observed the trail of the fox consisted of feathers; and knowing, or fancying there were no birds about in the winter, which the fox could get at, I was much puzzled for a time, but this spring threw a light on the subject. I found the small waterfowl, known to sailors as Mother Carey's Chicken, to others as the Stormy Petrel, in a dormant state, in a regular burrow, well feathered, and in good condition.

The discovery was made by mere accident. I had an excellent dog, with a fine nose—"a nose," as one of the skippers put it, "that would do credit to any health officer"—and finding him digging away at a burrow, I fancied I had a prize in the shape of a litter of young foxes, and perhaps the Vixen herself. So I signalled my companion, and we went to work, one holding a net and the other digging; the dog, with his tail wagging, with a subdued enthusiasm, anxiously awaited the result of our labour, ready to pounce on any animal that might make its appearance. The Labrador dog, let me remark, is a bold fellow, and, when well taught, understands, almost as well as any Christian biped, what you say to him. We were much disappointed with our labour, for, instead of a fox, we found about a dozen of these stinking birds. On their exposure to the sun, however, we were astonished to find animation soon returned, and most of them sought their native element—the water. I took some home with me, but they refused any sort of food, and died in a few days. The discovery of these birds had solved the problem—where did the foxes feed in the winter-time?

Now you may see animation once more along the coast, or at least in the bay. The homeward ship came in this year—for I have a particular year in view—as if by magic. We are fast approaching the middle of June and yet there are no Newfoundlanders on the coast, and the fish have not yet made their appearance owing to the jam of ice in the offing. This gives us more time for sport, for another cruize or two up the bay, to gather eggs or rinds, or to try and secure one of the large seals for bootbottoms for the ensuing winter, and to shoot a mountain-cat or two. These animals are not like the fox; if left on an island there they must remain, for they have a dread of water, and, never taking to it, fall an easy prey to the sportsman. But I have known a fox swim nearly a mile, and on one occasion I captured Reynard about half a mile on his journey to land.

The summer of this year I was much employed in coasting,* and mixed much with the Irish. I heard many a queer yarn from them,

---

* And, by the way, in various ways. For instance, I simply, but successfully, set a poor boy's broken leg, and made a will for one of the old hands. Thus was I captain, surgeon, and lawyer, in a single year.

related in their rich, humorous style. After the toil of the day is over, and the last meal is taken, no matter how tired a man may be, there are generally dancing and singing. I must say the Irish are indeed a happy, careless race! Wherever I have met them, I have invariably found them the same cheerful, mercurial set.

Being wind-bound in one of the northern harbours I met with a party similarly situated, and as we could not dance in a large open craft we "settled round" with pipes and tobacco, and each volunteered a yarn. As none of these yarns, however, have any connexion with life in Labrador, but nearly all related to the land of St. Patrick, the reader would not thank me for "padding" this little work with them. The story-telling faculty, however, which the Irish possess is, I may say, little less than a blessing to those who, as it were, are cut off from the world, and all but buried amongst the snows of Labrador. It whiles away the time, cheers the spirits, carries one back to the mother-country, and makes us " muse, and dream, and live again in memory." At the fireside, or under the clear cold stars, the Story Teller is attentively listened to and loudly applauded, his pipe re-kindled for him, and his flask re-filled.

While afloat on a coasting and trading voyage, I visited some old friends in St. Michael's Bay, and had the satisfaction of hearing the simple folks sing some of Watts' Hymns, copies of which I had left with them on a previous occasion. And let me remark at this point, that wherever the Gospel (without the trading missionary) has dawned upon the coast, the people —even the Esquimaux—have embraced it with cheerfulness. Indeed there is in this wild land a silent happiness which many a man and woman in England might envy: solitude without absolute loneliness, days of ease without care, nights of pleasure without parade. Thus year after year rolls on until death removes the sojourner, when, as his life has been spent in toil and labour, Eternal Rest falls upon him as a soft, sweet dream.

On leaving St. Michael's Bay I intended to return to the establishment "at home." But man is not his own master. It was a lovely morning when we left the bay, laden with the staple commodity of the coast, but we had not proceeded far when indications of a storm were observed in the eastern horizon. What should we do?

We were just then on a bold shore without any harbour under our lee. One of the old hands advised me to give the craft an offing, as he said, should the storm come easterly we could not weather the Cape, while, by putting her head off for an hour or so, we could easily manage it. Well the "schooner's" head was put to the eastward, both fore and aft sails were close-reefed, and the cargo was battened down; being first covered with tarpaulins, and then secured to the side of the schooner. Away we went under snug canvas, and for a time continued our course leisurely, but suddenly a puff came, carried away our foremast about ten feet from the deck, or carlins of the mast, and then the wind abruptly shifted to the south-west, and a strong gale arose. A heavy sea was also running at the time. None on board were prepared for this, as from the sudden shift of wind, instead of being well to windward, as we expected to have been, we were now dead to leeward of our island and in a crippled state. Luckily we had plenty of provisions on board, with a good supply of water, and I could not but think to myself, if the gale lasted, we should be carried in the course of a fortnight to England or Ireland against our will. It was fortunate for us the part of the mast which was carried away had—with the rigging—been saved. On examination I found the hooks of the runner stay had straightened from the sudden squall, and caused our mishap. In time we lashed the two stumps together, set our canvas anew, and hove the schooner to for the night, she gradually falling to leeward. On the morrow the gale seemed spent, and we made all sail we could, but to attempt to reach our island was out of the question, as we were dead to leeward of it.

In the course of the forenoon we found the wind had veered round to west, and so we determined to make for Newfoundland, and after three days' buffeting amongst the waves—three days of hard work and nervous anxiety—we found ourselves snug in a small harbour of that island.

CHAPTER XV.

NEWFOUNDLAND AND BACK AGAIN.

NEWFOUNDLAND is, like Labrador, proverbial for its hospitality to strangers. Indeed in all primitive countries the heart is kept open and formalities are thrown aside. Invitations are dispensed with. You hear pipe and tabor sound in a house, enter, and meet a welcome.

As we found the schooner had strained herself in the gale, and was making some water, it was necessary to have the cargo landed, and the hull examined and caulked. I thought therefore I would have a run on shore for a few days, and look about me. Being recognized by some of my old friends who had visited me on the coast, I was made more than usually welcome. One old skipper shook me by the hand, and said, "Well, my boy, you are come in the nick of time; we are about having an election of members for the Legislative Council, and rare fun it will be, for the members are elected by universal suffrage, while scarce a man-jack of the whole electors knows what universal suffrage means." Like that great philosopher, Mr. Pickwick, at Eatanswill, I looked forward anxiously for the election day; meanwhile, however, I enjoyed myself in a hundred ways—the evening dance, song, and story being, of course, the leading recreations.

The election truly was "good fun." Universal Suffrage seemed, with the Newfoundlanders, to stand for Universal Babel. A number of candidates were "up," but so determined were the electors to make the most of their privilege, that they wished to record their votes in favour of them all; and when this excessive liberality was objected to by the poll-clerks, many free and enlightened gentlemen declined to vote at all. "I'll vote for every one, or for no one!" was a common speech at the booths. To me the whole thing appeared a farce. The elective system was simply brought into contempt as—since the adoption of this same universal suffrage—I read it has been in our larger and more important colonies on the other side of the Pacific. Soon after the election my schooner was repaired, and all made ready for a start. On the morrow, after we were "fit for sea," a fine breeze sprang up from the south, and directly she felt the influence of the wind on her canvas, our little craft went bounding over the blue waters, and in three days we were snug in our small harbour.

The routine of the season was going forward as usual, and everybody congratulated us on our return. One fine Sunday afternoon, taking a stroll, as usual, after private divine service, I observed a long line of rowing boats—some fifty in number—pass the island. On inquiry I found it was an Irish funeral. A small island, about a mile from the main land, is consecrated for the burial of the believers in the Romish Church, and so particular are the Irish Catholics as to where they bury their dead, that they will ofttimes bring a body fifty or sixty miles for the purpose. Even should a person die in the winter, his or her remains are drawn to the island from an immense distance. One winter I was staying at a neighbouring establishment, when a man entered, and thus addressed the principal: "An God save ye! poor Paddy died last night, the Lord rest his soul!" at the same time crossing himself. "Well, Jem, what can I do for you?" was the reply. "Why, you see, sir, Bill and myself are about 'waking' the poor man, and we want a thrifle of rhum and brandy to wake him wid." "How many gallons will suffice?" "Oh! bedad, the matter of eight of rhum, and I could do wid four of brandy." "The quantity is too large for so small a crew." "Oh! sure, and we cannot do with less, and must have all the rhum, if not all the brandy." Well, eight gallons of rum and two of brandy were duly served out to "Jem," and away he went, rejoicing to think what a glorious wake they would have in the evening. Being curious to witness an Irish wake so far from the Old Land, I selected a companion, and away we went to the scene. Some few neighbours were invited, and kept up the wake until the rum and brandy were exhausted. Although

Jem was only a few hours in advance. the spirits had commenced their baneful influence. The coffin—which was in process of manufacture—was commenced with a regular elbow from the top, on one side, but before the other side was formed, the maker was so blind, he made it flat, and thus the coffin was constructed with three flat sides, and one with the usual elbow. Poor Paddy was often appealed to, to say if any of the present party had wronged him, and what for. Sometimes the corpse would be taken up, and, in drunken madness, embraced by one of his friends; then another would come up and dispute the right; then a scuffle would ensue, and the dead body would be thrust first in this corner, and then in that, but oftener would be laid flat in the middle of the floor. A little of this wake went a long way, and I speedily left the party, and walked home in the moonlight.

Being anxious, however, to learn the result of the affair, and to ascertain if any of the party had sustained injuries, I again visited the place in the morning, and found every one all but speechlessly intoxicated: when they spoke it was only to ask for more drink. I coffined poor Pat with great difficulty, as his limbs had become rigid with the frost. It was two days more before his countrymen were sufficiently recovered to take him to his last resting-place. The man just departed had some little property in nets, boats, and a small establishment on the coast, and (as we had no lawyers amongst us) these were fairly and quietly divided among his friends.

CHAPTER XVI.

LIFE ON THE COAST—AUTUMN.

We have a race on the coast who are thus curtly described by Cartwright in comparison with the honest and generous Esquimaux:—

> " Not so the mountaineers; a treach'rous race,
> In stature tall, but meagre in the face;
> To Europeans long have they been known,
> And all their vices these have made their own.
> Not theirs the friendly visit, nor the feast
> Of social intercourse; but like brute beast
> They greedily devour the recking meal,
> And then get drunk, and quarrel, lie, and steal."

To have a party of these marauders on your establishment is not at all pleasant. Their visits are certainly few and far between; for having no settled place of abode, they wander from locality to locality, catching furs and killing game for their support. When they have a sufficient quantity of furs to dispose of, they resort to the nearest establishment, and dispose of them for spirits, which they greedily swallow; they then have a fight amongst themselves, and when tired and well bruised, they spread out their deer-skins and sleep out their debauch. On awaking they will lie quiet, still shamming sleep; and, when they fancy the coast is clear, they rise from their affected slumber, and, if practicable, decamp with the very furs they had sold you. If they succeed in this, or any similar piece of felony, you have the consolation (if consolation it be) of knowing you will not see the same set of rascals again—or at all events for some years. They are fleet on foot, and expert marksmen, their weapon being the cross-bow, and a blunt arrow, so balanced that the top or blunt part just preponderates. They never aim direct at an object, but in a paraboloid—so well judging the altitude of the required curve that they seldom miss their mark. I saw the same feat performed with the blunt arrow which the Esquimaux did with the gun— I mean firing it perpendicularly in the air—the only difference being that the mountaineer never moved from the circle made, while so sure was his aim, that the arrow would fall at his feet, in front of him! Such bows and arrows are used by the natives of Siberia, and the same remarkable feat is performed by them.

There is another race of Indians on the coast; these are seldom seen, and are but little known, even to the natives. They appear at long intervals, and are called by the Esquimaux *Nascobi*. I never saw any of them, so, of course, I cannot describe them. I believe they and the mountaineers are mutual enemies, while the Esquimaux are the foes of both.

During my sojourn on the coast we had two visits from the mountaineers, but they conducted themselves so savagely that I was right glad to see their backs. The small dog spoken of in a former chapter is bred by this tribe. Although a wild and roving race, from the intercourse with Europeans they have imbibed all their "civilised" vices without one particle of their civilised virtues.

The fall of this year was charming. Indeed, November turned out finer than October, which gave us an opportunity of enjoying our favourite occupation—wild-fowl shooting, in the water. This year, with the mild weather, there came upon us innumerable quantities of small wild-fowl, called by the settlers "bull-birds." They are perfect ducks in miniature, and are web-footed; they seldom take wing, but keep continually skimming the water—now diving, and now rising again, with manifest enjoyment. Still, with all their efforts, they cannot evade man: I used to kill from thirty to forty of a morning.

One day, the sea being too rough for aquatic sports, I took my gun and strolled across the hills in search of wild-fowl along the different small inlets. On one of the hills I could command two or more of these inlets, and when I reached the summit I fancied I heard a piteous moan, as if from two or three dogs. Following the sound, I soon came upon the object which had attracted my attention. I found on a rock two dogs, half-a-dozen dead ducks, and a gun recently discharged. On my near approach, I recognised the dogs, and guessed who the missing party was. Nearing the animals, they showed their dislike to my disturbing any of the articles on the rocks. Still, one gently wagged his tail as if he knew me, and with a sorrowful expression of countenance—how dogs can express their grief or joy Sir Edwin Landseer has shown us—walked slowly to the edge of the rock, and, raising his head towards the sky, gave three of the most piteous moans I ever heard, and then returned and lay down to his charge. All I could do, I could not get the dogs to leave the spot. There they stood, as if still hopeful they would hear their master's voice again; but this they never did.

I marked the spot indicated by the dog, and retraced my steps homeward, and having to pass the man's hut who, I felt, had met a solitary death, I informed the remaining crew of my suspicions, and then I heard that their companion had set out in the morning for the place where I had found the dogs, having seen some birds about the spot the previous day, and wishing to shoot them.

The dogs remained at their post all night—no one could remove them. The next morning the sea was calm; three boats were launched, creepers placed in them, and off we went to the spot. I had no occasion to point out the place, for immediately on our approaching it, the dog who had moaned over the rock again did the same, and, after a short search near the spot, the body was found just under the cliff. On taking the corpse in the boat, both dogs commenced howling, and followed the boats to the Establishment, and would not leave their dead master until he was put under ground. Nay, for some days after, these two dogs haunted the grave, and, in whatever place they sat, kept their faces turned towards it, as if listening for the familiar call. An inquest was held amongst ourselves upon the body (as was our custom), and a verdict returned according to the evidence, which, although but circumstantial, clearly showed that, in the act of shooting, the poor fellow had fallen over the ledge of the rock.

On resuming my sport the day after the discovery of the body, I thought I had a rare prize in a large bird, standing some four feet high from the ground. I shot at and killed it, when, on picking it up, to my surprise I found it was a bittern—a bird nearly all neck, with a very small body. These bitterns are seldom met with in Labrador, and are even scarce in Newfoundland. I attributed its presence to the exceptional mildness of the season.

I may conclude this chapter by mentioning that one autumn we had a wreck on the coast, in consequence of a ship's compass being affected by, it was said, the juxtaposition of the vessel to a spot abounding in iron-ore. The captain had refused to take a pilot on board, but suddenly he found the compass-needle playing all sorts of antics—now describing a good half-circle, and now running right round the card. It may be that polar influences, rather than local metallic causes, were the reason of this. It is a subject on which I cannot attempt to pronounce. Certes, the vessel was wrecked, but the captain and crew were saved, and were well fed and clothed by the Good Samaritans of the far, far North.

CHAPTER XVII.

KING FROST AGAIN.

If every evil has its good, it would almost seem that every good has its evil. The mild November month threatens a severe frost for December, with little or no prospect of a "voyage of seals" for this year. Sure enough, as December came in, Nature at once grew rigid of demeanour, and the thermometer suddenly fell from fourteen to twenty degrees below zero. The seal-nets were placed out, but from the state of the weather were not sighted for more than a month afterwards. Although the climate of Labrador is so cold, sharks abound along the coast in the fall of the year, and many are entrammelled in the seal-nets. On clearing the nets, I found one of these monsters, measuring fourteen feet long, and well-proportioned; and, on opening him, I found quite a quarter of a hundredweight of fat inside of him—he having, as it were, peeled it off the seal as he fancied it.

One of the shipwrecked men saved from the schooner had been an ice-hunter, and whiled away many an hour by relating the mode of catching seals in the spring of the year on the coast of Newfoundland. At that time some three to four thousand men were employed in the capture in schooners of from seventy to two hundred tons' burden. The vessels were generally equipped by some of the merchants at the different ports, St. John's sending out the largest number. The crews vary from twenty to forty men, according to the size of the craft, and the ships are well found, with two rudders, and a false side to resist the pressure of the ice. These expeditions are fraught with considerable danger. It is absolutely necessary to keep leeward of the ice, as, should a gale come on and the craft be on the windward side, away goes the craft, false sides and all. Nothing can save it. If it is to leeward, and a close pack or jam of ice sets in, it is tolerably safe; the vessel becoming, as it were, set upon blocks, and there the crew await the "whelping" time. All young seals have white coats when whelped, but where they get their nourishment from for eight or nine days, I could never learn. Suffice it to say, in the course of that period they become quite fat, and fit to be taken or killed. They require but a slight tap on the nose, and are "settled." After a man has killed as many as he can conveniently walk off with, he drags them alongside the schooner, and walks off after another "turn," as it is termed; so that, if a craft happens to fall in with the main body, they may kill easily, for a crew of twenty men, some four thousand seals in about four days. These will yield from forty to fifty tons of oil. Some men, in their over-eagerness for gain, lose the whole of their catch. Before loading, a sufficient time must be allowed for the skin and fat of the seal to cool. The whole being put on board in bulk, should it not have "cooled," the entire mass heats, and becomes pure oil; and from the build of the Newfoundland crafts, they would fall on their beam-ends (as oil, like water, soon finds the centre of gravity), unless the liquid contents were pumped out again.

It frequently happens that a vessel will load in four or five days, run into port, discharge, and be in the ice again in ten days from the time she left it. I knew a skipper who had a famous dog for ice-hunting, and this would kill from thirty to forty old seals in the course of a day. Such an animal was a fortune to him, as he had only to feed him on the carcase, for which dogs have a remarkable fondness. I recollect one year's "return" of the seals killed on the ice. The number amounted to something like two hundred and thirty thousand.

The amphibious animal called the walrus is very rarely seen on the Labrador coast, and is rather a dangerous subject to encounter. It has no fear, and nothing less than a good gun will serve the purpose of getting rid of it. The tooth of the animal forms an ornament for the skirt of an Esquimaux cassock, and is supposed to take away all evil influence any person might have against the wearer.

K

About this time I was called on to visit a poor old man whose will I had made the previous year, and who was now on the point of death. I had often asked him to allow me to read to him, but he had invariably refused—saying he had lived through life without the Bible, and why could he not go out of the world the same? I never argued the point with him—why should I have done so? I thought to myself, when the old man wants me he will send for me, and I sha'n't refuse to go. When I saw him, he looked at me with an anxious eye, and, on asking him what were his wishes, he feebly and nervously replied, "I am not easy in my mind; I hope you have not taken amiss what I told you some time back: I should like you to read me something comforting. I have been a great swearer in my time, and feel I shall not be here long." I opened the Bible, and read to him from the fortieth chapter of Isaiah: "Comfort ye, comfort ye my people, saith your God." After finishing the chapter, which he listened to with much attention, he said how thankful he was for the cheering words of the Book, and hoped I would again visit him in the morning, which I promised to do. But when morning came, I found he was resting, with the calm look of an infant, in his last sleep! My next task was to read the Service for the Burial of the Dead over his remains. This done, I sold his effects by auction, and divided the proceeds as he had desired.

The bays were now fast—just like polished mirrors, and quite as slippery. Now was the time for skates, for the ice was so hard and smooth that an impression could not be made with the iron. In one of the harbours south it was nearly as severe as with us, and some of the youths, seeing the smooth ice, put the skates on and ventured from under the lee of the land. The moment they had gone so far, the breeze took the foremost of the party, and carried him, at mad speed, into a patch of clear water, where he was drowned—none of his companions daring to follow him, for fear of the same fate.

The celestial bodies in this part of the globe assume a special grandeur. The sky is so clear and the air so pure, while the moon at the full sheds so much light, you may, without difficulty, read the finest print by its lustre. Strolling on one of these fine nights, I observed the aurora borealis, but not clear, as the moon was too bright. On another occasion, however, when the moon was on the wane, I had an opportunity of witnessing the phenomenon from a height of three hundred feet above the level of the sea, and had a good chance of forming an opinion regarding it. In fact, it was—if I may so express myself—so close to me, I could distinctly hear a rustling noise as of sheets of paper being rubbed together. From what I saw then and on several subsequent occasions, it is my belief the aurora borealis is nothing more than a thin transparent vapour floating in the air, and acted upon by light currents of atmosphere, the celestial bodies reflecting themselves in and upon the vapoury veil. I never recollect seeing it with a strong wind blowing, but always in perfectly calm weather; and when we consider the rainbow, the lunar rainbow, the mock-suns, and the various other appearances of the same character produced by vapour, it is not unreasonable to classify the aurora borealis in the same category. But, whatever may be its cause, the aurora borealis is surprisingly beautiful, and seems like the portals of that City whose streets are of jasper. Meteors are very common in Labrador, and they are meteors always on the move and fond of sport. They dart and dazzle through the air like very Pucks.

This December I again started to explore the interior, taking with me the small team of dogs I possessed. On this excursion I was accompanied by two Esquimaux as guides, and we travelled sometimes fifty miles a day, but on other days we could not make more than five or six, and this with difficulty. Let me explain. You arrive at the foot of an island you have to cross; in crossing you save some miles, but the island is very steep all round, without any sign of vegetation—not even a stunted larch to assist you in ascending to the summit, which may be a hundred feet above you. Although you are provided with a small tomahawk or hatchet for the purpose of cutting steps to assist you, yet it frequently happens, after half-an-hour's toil, when you find yourself nearly at the top, your foot slips, and down you come to where you started from at the foot of the island. On our journey this necessity of cutting steps arose no less than three times in one stage. Of course, the fatigue is great, and after the toil you are glad to take rest in order to recover your strength. During this mode of travelling, when night comes on, you repair to the woods—that is, where there are any woods—fell the first trees, strip the boughs, which are converted into a sort of litter for sleeping on, and cut the timber into suitable lengths for your fire, which is mainly kindled to keep the wolves away;—not that I ever knew them attack men, but they might come and dispute about the provisions which you are compelled to carry for the day.

After three days' journey, we found ourselves snugly housed in the hut of a settler, who, as usual, showed us every hospitality, and here we stayed and made merry for three days and nights.

CHAPTER XVIII.

EXPEDITION TO SANDWICH BAY.

Early in the morning of the fourth day the dogs were harnessed, and away we started for the Isle of Ponds (distant about ten miles from the hut), where we heard there was a large herd of deer grazing. After ascending a steep hill, we came in sight of a boundless view many miles in extent, and, to my surprise, the Esquimaux informed me he could see the deer grazing some four miles off, and he even hinted how many there were. Descending the hill, we were fairly on the Isle of Ponds, with good hard snow to travel on. Very shortly the dogs got scent of the deer, and from this moment the sport and excitement commenced. The dogs tore along with the sledge at the wildest speed, in order to overtake the herd, regardless of the bumping and jolting we were receiving from the occasional unevenness of the snow. The deer, to the number of forty or fifty, all in line, bounded away for about two or three hundred yards, as they caught sight of us; then they faced about; then they darted off again for about fifty yards; and then, once more, halted. The shaking of the sledge made it impossible for us to take good aim, and, coming in contact with the stump of a tree, the sledge itself bounded into the air; the whole of us were thrown out, and away went the dogs on their own account in full chase. We were much annoyed at this, but late in the day we had the satisfaction of seeing the deer coming towards us, and the dogs in grand pursuit. This time we were more careful in our shooting. Lying down, we awaited their approach, and stopped one, which had also the effect of calling off the dogs, for, on his falling, they made for him directly. To skin the deer was the work of a quarter of an hour, and as fast as one took the skin off, the others were employed in cutting it up into joints. This was absolutely necessary, as it was freezing so hard that, had we not hastened our labour, the carcase would have become solid and difficult to carry, especially through the woods in deep snow. Even the skin was kept folded as the process of skinning was going on.

The deer scarcely relies for safety on its eyesight. It is provided with what the settlers call a "scrut-bottle," situated in the postern of the hind-leg, and containing a substance much like oil, which they smell, and which is so sensitive to the slightest atmospheric motion that it gives them notice of any danger to windward.

This day's sport led to another night in the bush, with keen appetite for our primitively prepared supper. A good fire having been kindled, and some long sticks cut to represent forks, slices of the venison were chopped off, and each man cooked his own according to his taste. Many an epicure would have envied us the meal had he known what a splendid sauce our hunger was. The Esquimaux took the heart of the deer, which, as it was frozen, was not considered to need cooking.

Throughout the night we were obliged to be vigilant and on the watch, as the wolves, scenting the savoury food, paid us near and numerous visits; but a shot every now and then kept them just beyond boundaries. Thus we passed the night, and with the sun took our departure north-west; and in the evening found ourselves again in comfortable quarters. They were certainly in the woods, but this time on the top of a hill some three hundred feet above the level of the sea. Here I saw some beautiful specimens of the flying squirrel, but being very nimble I could not catch one, and not belonging to the carnivorous species they are difficult to trap.

The establishments on this part of the coast are in some instances located at the foot of the hills, and the mode adopted to bring the wood for summer use to the sea-side is very curious. Two flat pieces of board, about six feet long by three inches wide, with a strap in the centre for the feet to go in, are worn by the woodmen to descend the hill, not the least exertion being used by them. With a heavy load on their backs, I have seen them slide down erect, and at almost railway speed. I must confess I was foolish enough to try my skill with a pair of these machines on my feet, and was rewarded with a bound of about ten feet down the hill, with sundry bruises for my pains.

The further north-west we went the more wood we discovered, and walked through many beautiful birch-groves. In the underwood may be found currants and raspberries, both very small, wortleberries and cranberries. The cherry also grows in some parts, but these are worthless, being without any flavour. The trees I mostly observed were the black, white, and red spruce, larch, silver-fir, birch, and aspen. The latter is valuable in Labrador on account of its durability under water. I saw one fine shrub, and was told it was called the "maiden-hair tea-shrub," used, when it could be found, as a substitute for our China tea—so *we* used it, and I must confess I liked the flavour quite as much as that of Souchong or Congou. The natives also use the spruce-boughs as tea. The only esculent (in the common sense) found on the coast fit to eat was named the " Alexander "— a species of celery. Scurvy-grass, young leaves of the osier, and of the ground wortleberry are, however, largely eaten. The "Alexander" is found in the crevices of rocks, where a small quantity of soil has been deposited, and the scurvy-grass is found at the river-heads of the different bays along the coast.

After a few days' shooting and hunting, we again started forward. Having proceeded a few miles, the dogs began to be restive; and, but for the activity of the Esquimaux, they no doubt would have given us another dance: but the Esquimaux overturned the sledge, and thus stopped their progress. On searching for the cause of this restiveness, we found the wolves had killed a deer, and four of them were discussing the hind and fore-quarters. As the wind was blowing from them, they were not aware of our approach, but the report of a gun sent them off growling, and left us part of their meal, which, although killed by the wolves, was not a whit the worse on that account.

The day was beautifully fine, with a Turneresque blue sky, the temperature at fourteen degrees below zero, and a shear-edged north wind. We came upon four deer, in the course of our journey, quietly grazing together, and apparently so listless that they allowed me to go up within an easy distance and despatch one.

Our next halt was at an Esquimaux wigwam. As usual, we found the women busy at work, while some of the men also were constructing "kyacks," or canoes for summer use. The timbers are made of the birch, steamed into the required shape, and are fastened together by strong lashings formed from the skin of the seal. Several seal-skins in the shape of the frame are then sewn together, and, when wet, are stretched over it, and the whole being secured, the "kyack" is entirely covered, save that an aperture is left in the centre to sit in. Although not more than eight or ten inches deep, the Esquimaux frequently convey their families from one place to another in these frail boats. I found one man employed in making a sledge. It was about twenty feet long by fourteen inches broad, the sides being formed of two-inch plank about a foot deep; the under-edges are shod with whalebone a quarter of an inch thick, fastened on with pegs made out of the teeth of the walrus. Across the upper edges are placed boards close together, and secured to the sides by means of strips of seal-skin. This sledge is called by the Esquimaux a "commeteck."

Leaving our friends, we again started across the barren waste, with nothing but ice and snow around us, and a compass to direct our course. Owing to an uncertainty as to whether we were on land or water, we made for the woods, and on our journey thither we found we were on the water, as many seals were sporting in the sun near their blowing-holes, and on our approach bored themselves through the ice in the most dexterous style. We had not the good fortune to catch a single one.

Another night in the bush. The day following brought us to Sandwich Bay. We here remained a week, each day exploring the interior as far as we could safely go. I found vegetation in this part much finer than elsewhere on the coast—in fact, all the trees and shrubs were larger. Game, too, was more abundant, and, although the winter was severe, fish could be caught in numbers. About twenty miles from the mouth of Sandwich Bay, inland and close to a place called Paradise, is a small lake about four miles long and two wide. In this lake may be found, summer and winter, an abundance of trout, salmon, and pike. In summer, nets are employed; in winter, holes are cut through the ice, and the hooks baited and let down. Thus you may fish your fill.

During my stay in this bay I visited the remains of an establishment originally founded by George Cartwright, so far back as 1792. He was very fond of Labrador, and spent a great deal of money in building and importing all sorts of birds and animals, with a view of getting them acclimatised; but he found the winters too severe. His exertions, however, were patriotic and unceasing;—for instance, he took out some greyhounds, but as the fall came on he saw their coats were not sufficient to keep them warm, so he had recourse to a flannel covering, only allowing the dog the use of its eyes. The hounds used to run about clad in woollen wrappers, but even with this protection they soon died.

Near this locality I found several Esquimaux had located themselves. As their wigwams were somewhat different from those I had before seen, I may as well describe one: the entrance was by a low, narrow passage, some twelve feet long and about three and a-half feet high, entirely formed of sods covered with snow. At the end of this passage was a square room of about fourteen feet, and lighted in the centre by a sort of skylight made from the entrails of the large seal. This was perfectly air-tight, and impervious to wet. The roof was formed in the same way as the passage, and round the skylight were flowers growing out of the whitened sods, like stars.

CHAPTER XIX.

JOURNEY HOME FROM SANDWICH BAY.

Leaving Sandwich Bay for our own home we made a détour to visit some other establishments before getting back. I have already remarked that the settlers in Labrador were hospitable in the extreme. I am sorry to say I found an exception to the rule in the man at whose establishment we next halted for the night. Perhaps our numbers alarmed him, as, although on setting out a month before we numbered but four, on our return homewards our party had grown to sixty, with a proportional increase of dogs. On nearing this man's habitation one or two hints were thrown out as to the sort of reception we should meet, but I could not believe that a man who had partaken of my hospitality the previous winter would refuse me his salt. Arrived at his house, however, we found him coolly standing at his door surveying our different movements. As we were unharnessing the dogs he called out, "How much farther are you going to-night?" "Why, we intend putting up here, at all events for the night, and as the weather is bad we shall have to stop." "Well then," said he, "I hope you have brought plenty of provisions with you." "No," said some one. "We heard what prime sport you had in the fall, and what a stock of deer you have buried. We come to pick a bit of it with you." The man growled his dissent, and declared he had none. Now everybody knows what a hungry Englishman is, and, as he refused to give, we reluctantly resolved to take. The dogs were set to find the buried venison, and in this they soon succeeded. Bulk was then broken—which means that the store was disturbed—and we were soon sawing and digging out a supply. When the carcass of the deer is stored up for winter use it is completely frozen, so some trouble is experienced to get any from the bulk. To disjoint it would be all but impossible. After a deer is taken out of bulk a cross-cut saw is procured, and the animal is sawed in two; the same is done with the fore and hind quarters, care being taken to gather the sawdust on a clean cloth, which proves a rich gravy. When the animal is cut up into quarters, a hand-saw is used to saw out steaks for the ever-hungry crew. Every one was soon amply provided with a supper on the occasion in question, while so numerous were we, that he who refused to give—who had meanly removed himself beyond the customs of the country—saw us take, and was powerless to interfere. But his parsimony cost him more than this. In such a country inhospitality is cruelty, and so his conduct was regarded by every one. No one would trade with him—no one even speak to him—and he lived the life of a hermit all the while he remained on the coast.

Being among the Esquimaux I was curious to learn how the icebergs were formed, and made inquiry of many. Still it was some time before I could assure myself their theory was correct. One intelligent old man explained their formation to me nearly in the following words:— The immense islands of ice—for they are nothing less—which you daily see on the coast of Labrador, or, at all events, near the coast, can only be formed in this manner. The sea in the extreme north is of such a depth that navigators have often not been able to find the bottom with a line of a hundred fathoms; even close to the shore the land is very high, and many parts of the shore are perpendicular. The face of the coast being greatly broken, numbers of bays and coves are formed, and these are defended from any swell rolling into them from the sea, by the prodigious quantity of flat, low ice, which almost continually covers that part of the ocean, and which, it may be presumed, prevents those bays and coves from breaking up for one, two, or more years together. The severe frost of our winter will form flat ice upon them of an incredible thickness; that ice is deeply covered with the snows which are constantly falling, and a thousand times more is drifted upon it from the adjoining land, until the accumulation is beyond estimation or conception. On the return of summer the sun and rain cause the snow to become wet and to shrink together, when the frost from beneath, striking up through the whole mass, consolidates it into a firm body of ice. In this manner it keeps continually accumulating, until the adjoining sea gets clearer of drift-ice than usual, when a gale of wind sets in from the southward, sends in a swell which breaks up the whole and divides it in many pieces, resembling huge white rocks, flushed with soft blue, which are slowly dragged to the southward by the current. As several of those islands may be some years before they arrive in a climate that is capable of dissolving them, it is more than probable that in the mean time they gain more in the course of each winter than they lose in the intermediate summer.

Cartwright supports our part of this theory, for he observes " that when they have advanced some distance to the southward, they thaw so much faster under water than they do above it, that they lose their equilibrium, upset, and fall in pieces; otherwise," he adds, "I verily believe that some of them would drive almost to the equinoctial line before they were entirely dissolved."

After our night in the bush, and our dismemberment of the deer, we moved on for home. On passing some of the islands I had visited the year before, I found their character quite changed. The weight of ice and snow on many a point had levelled the whole to the ground. I have often observed, in journeying to the north in severe winters, the snow lies so deep that perhaps for two or three years objects such as boats, huts, timber, and it may be, human beings, will be concealed by it. The next year comes a mild season, the objects so buried come to light, and the whole aspect of the place is changed. I have frequently passed a spot where I knew sundry boats to be buried, but, from the depth of snow and ice over them, they could not be got out. Let a hope come from this to the relatives and friends of long-missing Arctic travellers. I have missed well-known objects — well-known men — for several years, and then a warmer season than usual has melted the walls of snow and ice by which they were surrounded.

Travelling in Labrador in the winter-time is, although cold, pleasant enough. You have lots of warm clothing on, and other means of coping with the severity of the season. In the summer months, however, it is not so cheerful. The traveller must carry all his provisions on his back, together with his hatchet, and from the continued interruptions of lakes and rivers he will find, if he has a "crow's distance" of five or six miles to go, he must generally perform a journey of at least ten to fifteen miles, with the ground giving way under his feet, as if walking on sponge, to say nothing of the intolerable and incessant torment of millions of flies. Indeed when an early spring appears, so great is this last plague, that the furrier who has to collect his traps, placed out since the last fall, is really compelled to take another hand with him to combat the flies. They light a quantity of green wood, fill an iron pot with it, and then, placing the pot on the centre of a pole some ten feet long, each takes an end, and thus they trudge on through the bush, the smoke almost blinding them, but keeping the flies at a distance.

With all these drawbacks life is enjoyed on the coast. Cartwright used to say, he thought Labrador would make a capital settlement for convicts; the only thing wanting was snug quarters for the chief of the department and his subordinates. Is this idea still worth consideration? I think it is.

CHAPTER XX.

HOME AGAIN.

NOTHING particular befel us on our return homeward. Every one seemed pleased with the trip, and as we left each other to proceed to our respective establishments, a hearty shake of the hand all round showed that good-fellowship prevailed amongst us. It was strange what a change had been wrought in the appearance of some of us! I found, what I had often been told, that the wind and frost tan the skin much more than does a tropical sun; so when I came home my men did not recognize me, but mistook me for some coloured savage.

Never having properly " gone to bed " for a month—during which time I had been away—I thought I should enjoy my first night's " bed " again amazingly. I was, however, greatly disappointed, for, after lying down some time, I was seized with a suffocating sensation, and had to dart into the open air to get my breath. After my long encampments beneath the moon a real feather-bed was for a long time unendurable.

The day after my arrival I had a visit from an old acquaintance. The black bears had been and played him a trick in the fall of the year, with his olive oil, and stolen the most part, so he wanted a small supply to make good the loss. How much did he want? Oh! only about two gallons. On inquiry I found the open stock was expended, so, sending for the carpenter and his mate, we proceeded to the oil-store, and selected a butt, and cut it in two with a saw.

Then with mallet and chisel we carved out the quantity required, weighed it, packed it up in brown paper, and gave it to the purchaser, and away he went towards home. On his arrival the wife, having dinner nearly ready-prepared, asked if he had the oil, as she wanted it as a sauce for the fish. "Sure an' I have," said Pat, and put his hand under his stiffly-frozen blanket-frock, to produce it from an inner pocket, when, to his astonishment, he found only the sheet of brown paper which had contained the oleaginous block! The oil itself was not to be found. A light then instantly broke upon the shrewd housewife, and she requested her husband not to come too near the fire, and bade him change his clothes. This he did, and the wife having hung them up before the fire, and placed a pan beneath, nearly the whole of the oil was caught in it. The oil had melted with the air-tight heat of Pat's coat, and run down his clothes, where it had again frozen, and the stiff, cumbrous nature of the dress had prevented him noticing either process. Pat used to say, " Bedad I was startled when I found it had gone; but when Biddy sent me upstairs to put on fresh clothes, and I came back and spied the oil in the pan, I said, ' Get out wid ye! you're a witch!' "

The spring was passed as in former years, and presently the outward ship from home arrived.

It happens that when ice is scarce in the United States, schooners frequent the coast for the purpose of obtaining a supply for the West India Islands. The mode of procuring it is attended with much risk to the adventurers: a small iceberg, grounded near the shore, is selected, the schooner sails alongside, and the crew work night and day until the craft is loaded. This takes only a short time, but the danger is great, as should the top of the iceberg become heavier than the part under water, away goes schooner, crew and all. I had an opportunity of witnessing a schooner loading—or rather about to load—in this way from a berg; and just as the crew had made the vessel fast and commenced, crack it went, and turned over. The act was so sudden that the crew had not time to cast off their grapples, to save the craft from being taken some ten feet out of water, when fortunately the hawsers broke, and down she came with the loss of both masts. Fortunately no lives were sacrificed, the whole affair not lasting more than five minutes. There is never the least notice given, nor any perceptible index afforded, that an iceberg is turning over. To replace the schooner's masts was only the work of a few days, when, to my surprise, I found the crew once again engaged in their perilous occupation upon another berg.

Labrador abounds in white spar, and also in small specimens of that beautiful one called "Labrador spar;" but from the action of the snow and ice lodging in the crevices of the cliffs during the winter, tons of rocks are every spring of the year split asunder, and fall into the sea, so that any mining operations near the coast would be impossible. Ironstone may also be found along the shores in large quantities, but the prosecution of fishing and sealing yielding good profit, less remunerative employments are naturally neglected. On a small island, in 51° 21' N., and 55° W., I have often observed on the easternmost point the subsoil covered with a black sort of stone resembling coal, and have frequently taken portions home with me and placed it on the fire, and found it to give a strong heat much like the culm of South Wales. From the looseness of the subsoil I have thought a good mine exists on this island, which could easily be worked in the summer, while the produce could be drawn away to the main during the winter months, as it would be impossible for any ship to anchor near it in the summer-time. The harbour, being formed by two small islands bearing east and west, opens to the ocean, and from the directions I have given the spot may be readily found by the ships of any enterprising company desirous of testing the mine—if mine there be.

CHAPTER XXI.

TRAINED DOGS AND HOMEWARD BOUND.

During winter, for want of horses, dogs are used for the purpose of conveying all sorts of produce to and from the bays, as well as for pleasure. Some are trained as retrievers, watch, house, and water dogs. Still they are all of the same breed. The retriever is well known in England, but I fancy the duty of the Labrador watch-dog is little if at all understood. In the summer and fall, then, many stray ducks may be seen frequenting the small bays round the islands; the watch-dog lands with you, and, with much caution, examines the shore, and directly he observes ducks, he will instantly lie down and crawl out of their sight, then immediately rise and run towards you, when by his actions you may be sure he has sighted a company. He leads the way, and when in the vicinity of the birds, down he crouches, and you must do the same. Should you be over-eager, and fire at too great a distance, and miss your birds, the dog looks towards them for a moment, as if reflecting!—" It's no use going into the water, he has not killed any,"—and stands still. If, on the other hand, you have a good shot—killing, say, half-a-dozen, and crippling three or four—in he bounds, leaving the dead birds and giving chase to the cripples. If they are wounded in the wings they swim with difficulty, and cannot dive, and so become an easy spoil. The dog has the instinct to know this, for he wastes but little time in the pursuit. It constantly arises that the spot from whence the ducks are shot is, at least, ten feet perpendicular from the water; sportsmen provide themselves in such instances with what is termed a "gunning gaff," some twelve feet long, with an iron crook at the end, made in the shape of a shepherd's crook. The dog brings a duck at a time under the rock; you place the crook round its neck, and draw it up or land it. The last bird the dog retains in his mouth, and allows himself to be drawn up in a somewhat scientific manner; that is to say, having seized the bird firmly across the wings he swims under the rock, and allows his master to place the hook through his collar at the back of the neck; then placing his paws against the rock, and throwing his weight on the gaff, he gracefully walks up and lands his game; did he not retain it in the operation in all probability he would be choked.

Of a fine day I have seen these dogs near the landwash amusing themselves fishing, diving six or seven feet, and bringing up a fish every time. Their mode of diving is not direct, but spiral.

It has been said a goose is a foolish bird, and certainly the geese of Labrador are very foolish indeed. They are found some miles up the bays, and when discovered the dog uses a simple artifice to decoy them. Near the shore (the neighbourhood of a small wood, with goose-grass in the foreground, is their favourite resort) he rushes out of the wood into the water and swims some eight or ten yards, with head low and tail out—looking something like a water fowl—then comes back to the shore, and so continues until he fancies they are within shot, when he quietly waits by your side watching your gun, and, by his looks, showing his anxiety to see the flash. Then off he goes and secures his birds, and lands them at your feet.

The house-dog has a peculiar sagacity. I

trained one to keep house in a noiseless manner. If myself or steward was not at home, and a visitor called, the dog would allow him to walk in, sit down, light and smoke his pipe, as if unconscious of his presence; but if the visitor attempted to leave the house the dog was up in an instant, and, placing himself in the doorway, showed a set of teeth of dazzling but appalling whiteness. The frightened fellow again returns and takes his seat, the dog once more lies down, and thus the pair are seen on the return of one of the household. A visitor once served that way takes care to look through the window on his next call, to see if any one is at home. The dogs sent to England, with rough shaggy coats, are useless on the coast; the true-bred and serviceable dog having smooth, short hair, very close and compact to the body. I sent to England a fine specimen of these, but unfortunately the vessel which bore it had the misfortune to be wrecked on the north coast of Ireland, and all hands were lost.

Before leaving the coast I met with an accident which nearly cost me my life; as it was, it deprived me of the sight of one eye (fortunately the left one). Learning that a stray deer had been seen on an island about four miles off, I started in pursuit of it, and after gaining the spot came in view of the desired object, examined, loaded my rifle, and took a deliberate aim, when, instead of the deer falling, I found myself tottering backwards. The crew I had with me placed me in the boat and conveyed me with all speed to my home.

On my arrival I found I had lost much blood, and, calling for my writing-desk, commenced writing to my friends in England how my last moments had come to pass, which, at that time, I expected to be near at hand. I had written about half-a-dozen lines, when the pen fell from my grasp, and all consciousness left me. I was in that state for some days, when, on recovery, I found an old nurse and her daughter anxiously watching my return to sense. As is common in such cases, my first inquiry was, what had happened? when the whole was explained to me. The rifle had burst, and the ball had passed in a retrograde direction, striking my left temple, and grazing it about the sixteenth of an inch, opening the veins in that region of the head. Although no doctor was there, every attention was paid me, and in about six weeks I was all right again.

Some of my Irish friends learned I was about leaving the coast in the fall of the year, and on parting with the " early-leaving ones "—as the first ship of passengers is called—many a hearty wish was expressed by my demonstrative friends for a safe passage to myself across the water, and many a hope that the following spring would see me once more amongst them. On the day of my departure I received no less than twelve large loaves of new-baked bread, as tokens of regard from them. The night before my departure was spent in merry-making, and a right jovial time we had of it. While in Labrador I only met with one Scotchman, and not even with one Welchman.

Three of the old hands, who had not visited England for more than twenty years, took passage with me. The brig we embarked in was about two hundred tons, oil-laden, and in good trim. The master, however, was a timid old man, declaring he should not press his brig with too much canvas; and to be on the right side he actually stowed away his top-gallant masts under the cargo, "because," as he put it, "it was best to keep out of temptation!"

This fall, winter had set in early and severe, and we were not one day too soon under weigh. The first night the drifting mist was freezing as fast as it reached the cordage, and the deck of the brig was, on starting, almost a mass of ice, and the rigging three or four times its original size. A sort of artificial gallery ran all round the ship. After three or four days at sea this disappeared, but, in detaching itself from aloft, it came rattling down much to the discomfort of the crew and passengers. During all this time the old skipper kept watch in the companion, and nothing could persuade him to venture on deck after the fifth day. Signs of rough weather then made their appearance, and it commenced blowing in sudden puffs and squalls, much to the amusement of the crew, who said, so long as we had the gale, the old skipper would keep below and not annoy them. "For," said an old salt, "you see, sir, interest in the merchant-service is like that in the navy: they all look out for their relations. The skipper is related to the owners, and the mate sails the ship." The old man continued: "I have sailed in several men-of-war, and I don't know how it was, but hang me if nearly all the captains and some of the officers did not belong to the same family, as if a whole tribe, sir, was born tip-top sailors!"

The wind increasing, orders were given to heave the brig to, although the wind was right aft. Presently the gale became a perfect hurricane, the brig driving home stern foremost. On the third day, after heaving to, a sea struck her on the starboard bow, carrying away all the bulwarks, and this was followed by another, sweeping the deck of the cabouse, or cook-house, with sundry casks of water, "right away." Fortunately the crew saw the sea coming and secured themselves; as luck would have it the masts held on fast. It was now certain that we should be short of water, and all hands were immediately placed on half-allowance. It was always a shame that ships, even when making short voyages, should be permitted to carry their stock of water in casks ranged along the side of the deck. In our case we were, in consequence of the casks having been carried away, so short of water that one man exchanged a bottle of it for a bottle of spirits. It was an unfortunate bargain for him. He drank the spirits, was seized with thirst and fever, and died.

We had been hove to for six days, with only bread and water and a small quantity of spirits to eat and drink, when the wind moderated and enabled the crew to wear ship and set more sail; also to get a fire "under weigh," and thus to enjoy a warm meal. We had been out now eleven days, and as we were so short of water, and as the wind still continued favourable, the mate persuaded the master to carry more sail. This was done, and at the end of eight days we were steering for an anchorage at St. Mary's Island (Scilly). As this was Sunday we returned thanks for our safe deliverance from the perils of the deep, and, I must say, enjoyed a draught of pure water with more zest than if it had been Constantia or Champagne. We then went on shore and made merry.

When the reader remembers that some of us had not seen a " house," in the English sense of the word for twenty years, he will sympathise with the liberal use that was made of the cosy inn parlour and a thousand other comforts upon shore. The sight of a real four-post bedstead was nothing less than inspiriting.

Next day we were again on board the brig. We had a splendid north-west breeze, and, in a few days, were safely anchored in a snug little harbour on the coast of Devon. I cannot express my joy on again returning to my native land, but as the reader closes this little work let him think of the hard life I had led and the dangers I had undergone, and conceive for himself all the feelings I find it impossible to set upon paper.

THE END.

www.ingramcontent.com/pod-product-compliance
Lightning Source LLC
Chambersburg PA
CBHW020804230426
43666CB00007B/853